CONFUCIUS

CONFUCIUS

A BIOGRAPHY

JONATHAN CLEMENTS

SUTTON PUBLISHING

First published in the United Kingdom in 2004 by
Sutton Publishing Limited · Phoenix Mill
Thrupp · Stroud · Gloucestershire · GL5 2BU

British Library Cataloguing in Publication Data
A catalogue record for this book is available from the British
Library.

ISBN 0-7509-3322-4

Typeset in 11.5/15pt Melior
Typesetting and origination by
Sutton Publishing Limited.
Printed and bound in England by
J.H. Haynes & Co. Ltd, Sparkford.

for
Fred Patten

Contents

List of Illustrations

(Between pages 74 and 75)

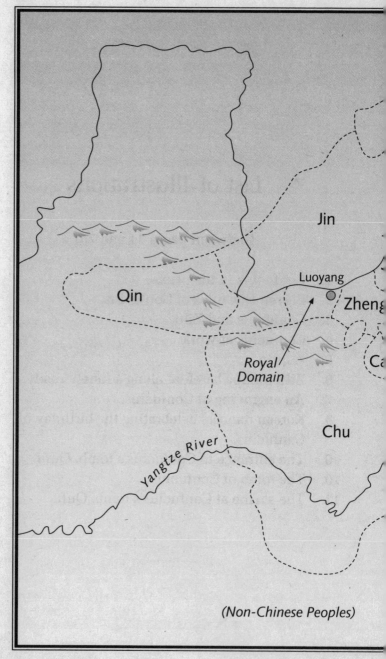

China at the time of Confucius

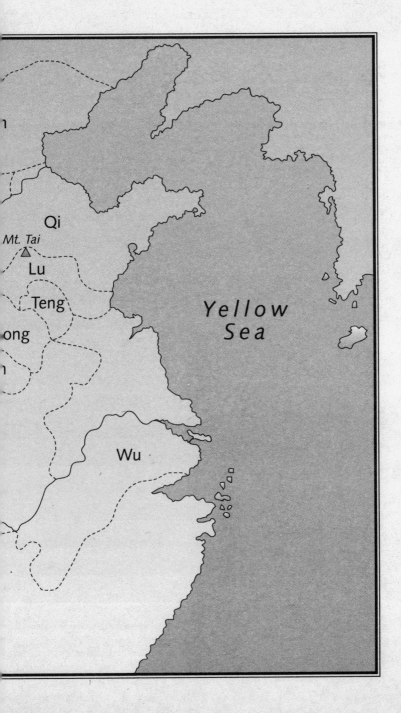

Chronology

c. 551 BC Birth of Confucius – 28 September 551 is commonly accepted as the official date.

c. 547 Death of Confucius's father.

c. 541 The Shining Duke becomes the ruler of Lu.

c. 531 Confucius marries.

c. 530 Confucius gains employment as manager of a state granary. Birth of Confucius's son, Li, also known as Boyu, or Top Fish.

c. 529 Confucius promoted to state husbandry manager.

c. 528 Confucius begins teaching.

c. 527 Death of Confucius's mother.

c. 520 Confucius meets the Honoured Duke, ruler of the neighbouring state of Qi.

c. 518 Meng-xi of the Mengsun clan on his deathbed recommends the promotion of Confucius.

c. 517 Confucius visits the royal capital, Luoyang.

c. 516 After a conflict breaks out in Lu, Confucius is forced to relocate briefly to Qi.

c. 511	Confucius possibly begins compiling the *Book of History* and the *Book of Songs*. Birth of Yan Hui, Confucius's cousin and favourite disciple.
c. 510	Death of the Shining Duke in exile.
c. 510	According to some sources, Confucius divorces his wife.
c. 510?	Confucius allows his daughter to marry Gong Ye-chang.
c. 501	Confucius becomes the chief magistrate of Zhong-du.
c. 500	The Decisive Duke makes Confucius assistant to the assistant-superintendent of public works. Confucius's diplomacy at a summit saves his lord's life.
c. 499	Confucius becomes Minister of Justice.
c. 497	Confucius resigns.
c. 496	Confucius heads east to Wei, and then to the border, where he is mistaken for his old enemy Yang Hu.
c. 495	Confucius travels between several Chinese states.
c. 493	Death of the Spirit Duke in Wei.
c. 490	Death of the ruler of Qi, the Honoured Duke.
c. 491	Confucius travels to several kingdoms in the region, but is unable to find prolonged employment.
c. 485	Death of Confucius's wife.
c. 484	Returns to Lu after the successes of his disciple Ran Qiu. Presumably begins

editing and adapting Lu's state history, the *Spring and Autumn Annals*.

c. 483   Death of Confucius's son Top Fish. Supposed birth-date of Confucius's grandson Zisi.

c. 481   Confucius aged seventy. Supposed capture of a *qilin* in western Lu.

c. 479   Death of Zilu during a revolution in Wei. Death of Yan Hui.

c. 479   Death of Confucius.

213   Qin Shi Huangdi, the First Emperor of China, orders the Burning of the Books.

206   The new Han dynasty adopts Confucianism as its state philosophy.

1 AD   Pingdi, the Emperor of Peace, confers ducal rank on Confucius in the afterlife.

57   Imperial colleges begin to offer sacrifices to Confucius.

492   During the reign of Wudi, the Martial Emperor, Confucius is given the title 'Accomplished Sage'.

609   Confucius becomes the subject of veneration in dedicated temples.

1645   Shunzhi, the Emperor of Unbroken Rule, proclaims Confucius to be 'the Ancient Teacher, Accomplished and Illustrious, the Perfect Sage'.

1704   Pope Clement XI forbids Chinese Catholics to perform rites in honour of Confucius or their ancestors.

1906	Guangxu, the Emperor of Shining Sequence, decrees that sacrifice to Confucius should be undertaken at the same level as sacrifice to Heaven and Earth.
1912	Abdication of the Last Emperor.
1949	Establishment of Communist rule in China. Confucian values are challenged as patriarchal and oppressive.
2004	Confucius's 2,555th birthday. Six million people describe themselves as 'Confucianists'. Another 379 million follow his teachings.

Introduction

They who set their hearts on doing good, will
be forever free from evil. *ANA*: IV, 4

Everybody knows of Confucius, but few know much
about him. Few Westerners are likely to know a
single one of his sayings, even though he is the most
important philosopher in Chinese history, whose
legacy continues to this day. There are six million
people in the world who describe themselves as
'Confucianists', while the Chinese belief system that
Confucius helped preserve has 379 million followers
in 91 countries (6.4 per cent of the world's population, compared to the 6 per cent who are Buddhist).
Confucius has also attracted followers outside
the Chinese sphere of influence, particularly in
America, where his teachings are seen as a prag-
matic, benevolent system of ethics that does not
require religious faith.

Though he is often revered as semi-divine, Confucius himself had little time for thoughts of the

supernatural. For him, there was no need for talk of retribution or rewards in a nebulous afterlife. Instead, Heaven or hell began in the here and now, with those around us. Husbands had a duty to their wives, the old to the young, and parents to their children. If each remained benevolent, while the other remained obedient, these simple rules would extend out into the wider world, augmenting relationships between rulers and subjects, teachers and students, or ourselves and our friends.

However, this teaching is often interpreted as an incontrovertible rule, whereas it incorporates another important aspect of Confucianism – obligation. The emphasis here is on relationships, not hierarchies. In India, for example, it would be argued that a wife must endure whatever hardships her husband should subject her to, simply because such troubles are fated to be her *karma*. Not so in Confucianism, where it is the husband's *duty* to love and to cherish. For Confucius, tyranny of all kinds was 'worse than a man-eating tiger', and each half of any relationship is obliged to honour and respect the other. People were expected to know their place, but also to acknowledge that the higher had responsibilities of its own towards the lower.

Confucius called this obligation the Mandate of Heaven. Heaven has ordained a difference between right and wrong, and true believers must always do what they truly believe to be right. Today, we rarely hear more than a fragment of the Mandate – it is rarely mentioned except in reference to the divine authorisation of the Chinese emperor to rule. But the Mandate stretches far beyond that – the emperor only rules for as long as he serves his subjects. The Mandate is easily revoked in the face of bad deeds or unjust behaviour, and Confucius believed that previous bad rulers had been deposed through the withdrawal of Heaven's support.[1]

Confucius saw no harm in acting out of kindness; he sought to make the world a better place by preaching righteousness at a personal level. In his ideal world, goodness between the members of the family would expand into kindness between neighbours, into truth within a community and ultimately a benevolent world. Such was the teaching and belief of Confucius.

There are few biographies of Confucius, and those that do exist often tend to collapse into discussions of his philosophy rather than his life. This is chiefly because hardly any of his biographical details are certain. The largest source, *The Analects*, was assembled long after his death, as were all other books in which he is quoted. One supposedly comprised personal memories of the master, but, if other sources are to be believed, the author was barely four years old at the time of Confucius's death. In writing this book, I have walked a dangerous line between fact and supposition. I have outlined the bare bones of Confucius's life, and trawled through the available sources in an attempt to place the disordered quotes in a chronological order.

I have worked from facsimiles of the original ancient texts, as well as commentaries in modern Mandarin and English. There are several forms of 'Confucian' saying: the words of the Master himself, others' wisdom which he quoted himself, the words of others quoting him, and more apocryphal sayings that are merely attributed to him.[2] I have taken extracts from the most famous books in which his disciples wrote down his words. The *Analects* contain twenty books of direct quotes and reported dialogues between Confucius and his followers. Two other books thought to contain the essence of Confucian teaching are the *Doctrine of the Mean*, compiled by Confucius's grandson, and the *Great Learning*, compiled by a pupil.[3] This book also includes references to *The Essentials* and a few sections from *Several Disciples Asked*, from a 'new' Confucian manuscript that was found in an ancient Chinese grave in 1973, and published in recent years.[4] I have also consulted the Confucian anecdotes in the *Book of Rites*, and the *Kong Family Masters' Anthology*, a doubtful source believed to date from the early centuries of the Christian era.

Classical Chinese is a remarkably terse language designed to summarise the spoken word rather than reproduce it, and I have expanded where necessary for clarity. An original statement, such as 'SELF WHAT NOT WANT NO DO AT MAN' (*Analects*: Book XV, Chapter 23) cannot be left in its original compressed form, but needs to be unravelled into the vernacular, just as the Chinese would do themselves. The end result: 'Treat others as you yourself would like to be treated', or even 'Do as you would be done by' should, I hope, make Confucius far more accessible.

Few facts are solid. Even his birthday is widely disputed, and often we can only guess the date of certain scenes by incidental details. Despite these problems, I have done my best to keep to my publisher's brief, and to strip away centuries of commentary to reveal something much simpler – the troubled life of a teacher who lived two-and-a-half thousand years ago. Wherever possible, I have used the original sources to tell the story in his own words, only adding brief bridging sections to explain some of the backgrounds of the events under discussion.

Chinese is a rich and many-layered language, reduced to meaningless monosyllabic grunts when written in the Latin letters of the upstart Roman Empire. Over the centuries, the great tragedy of East–West understanding has lain in the fundamental difficulty of translating between these two very different language families. I have carefully shifted any superfluous Chinese words into the notes, where they will not complicate the text any more than is necessary. I feel the pain of the non-specialist reader forced to make sense of a sentence like: 'Kong left Qi for Lu, where the Ji held sway', and have done my best to simplify matters with semi-translations. On many occasions, I have mixed what translators call communicative and referential language – in other words, I have written what things *mean*, rather than what they say.

Rather than burden the reader with characters' birth-names, nicknames, given names, surnames, poetic names, honorifics and posthumous names, in three or four contradictory romanisation systems, none of which will mean a thing to a non-specialist, I have simply chosen one and stuck with it. It is better, surely, that we know Confucius's first patron by his posthumous title, the Shining Duke,[5] than it is to force a general audience to memorise several appellations or changes in rank through his lifetime. Glosses for the original Chinese names and variant romanisations can be found in the notes at the back of this book, where any readers who wish to be driven slowly mad may enjoy them at their leisure.

Also, I have referred to the subject of this book as Confucius, even though the name was only created by European Jesuit scholars some 2,000 years after his death – their attempt to Latinise *Kong Fuzi*, 'Master Kong'. The word 'Confucianism' is also a Western invention.

In his day, Confucius was merely regarded as the latest and most proficient in a long scholarly tradition that stretched back for centuries. But Confucius refined that tradition and codified its principles, creating a system for looking at the world that would eventually come to bear his name.

1

Ancestry and Early Life

At fifteen, I set my mind on learning. *ANA*: II, 3

Three thousand years ago, there was a war at the centre of the world. The powerful Shang people had ruled for centuries after overthrowing a former tyrant. Now, the ruling tribes of the Shang warred against the neighbouring land of the Zhou, and were beaten back. After a while, the Zhou peoples realised that their victory was a sign of military superiority over the supposed rulers of the world, and went on the offensive. The Zhou people overthrew the Shang, and plundered the treasures of their royal city. They proclaimed that they were the new kings, and that Heaven had willed it by allowing them to defeat their former oppressors.

The Learned King, and his son, the Martial King, were revered as great heroes, but their domain was too large to rule single-handed. Instead, they parcelled out areas of land to their greatest warlords and most loyal servants, creating a series of dukedoms across much of what is now known as northern China. In the early Zhou dynasty the feudal lords obeyed their rulers, and, supposedly, the world entered an enlightened age.[1] As time went by, the semi-independent lords gained their own resources and armies, and eventually became more powerful than their nominal rulers. Within 300 years, the Zhou kings were a shadow of their former selves, huddled in a tiny royal domain. Their capital of Luoyang was regarded as a centre of cultural excellence, but the power of the kings was weak indeed. The kings were 'sons of Heaven' charged with ruling the world on behalf of the distant gods. For as long as they did not try to exert their authority too much, their former vassals continued to pay lip-service to them.

The words we use to describe the life of Confucius, like 'king', 'book', and 'city', sometimes serve to mislead us with their very familiarity. When Confucius was born, Rome was still a collection of huts. Pythagoras had yet to develop his theory of geometry, Buddha was still not enlightened, and Jerusalem had yet to build its fabled Temple. Cambyses II ruled the Persian Empire, from where he coveted Pharoah Ahmose II's Egypt. The attempted Persian invasion of the West, that would unite the Greek city-states and lead to European civilisation as we know it, was still forty years away. The Zhou kings, who believed themselves to be the rulers of the whole world, were largely ignorant of these other civilisations. As far as they were concerned, there was the Middle Kingdom, where they ruled, and then there were barbarians waiting for the light of civilisation.

There is no need to discuss something that has already been done. There is no gain in scolding for an act that has already finished. There is no point in blaming anyone.

ANA: III, 21, iii

China in the sixth century BC was not the monolithic state of recent centuries, but a cluster of interrelated dukedoms. The nominal king dwelt in a small area near the upper reaches of the Yellow river. Radiating out from the royal domain were thirteen principalities that paid homage to their symbolic leader, but were largely left to govern themselves. These in turn were often subdivided into smaller baronies and city-states. Their ruling families indulged in unending squabbles over succession and territory.

Sources differ on how far the ancestry of Confucius can be traced into the past. He certainly believed that he was a distant descendant of royalty. However, the blue blood in Confucius's veins came from the long-defeated line of the previous dynasty. The lost kingdom of Shang had been a small state encompassing the floodplain of the Yellow river.[2] When the Zhou had seized control, the last Shang king remained wilfully ignorant of the disaster faced by his country, but his elder half-brother,[3] the son of a royal concubine, decided that it was time to cut his losses. Rather than stay for the inevitable end, the half-brother withdrew from the court, leaving his more belligerent relatives to resist their superior enemies.

He was eventually rewarded for his non-combatant stance. With the Zhou now ruling both their own territory and the conquered state of the Shang, the pacifist was co-opted into the new nobility. He was given the principality of Song over which to rule and was charged with continuing the ancestral sacrifices to the departed members of the Shang royal family. By this means, the new rulers hoped to appease the vengeful spirits of the rulers they had overthrown. As Confucius's most famous and high-ranking fore-father, this man would have been the subject of some family pride. Whereas a more military-oriented family could have regarded such an ancestor's act as appeasement or collaboration, the relatives of Confucius regarded it as an act of honourable pragmatism. Nor would it be the first time that one of Confucius's ancestors found themselves turning away from violence and political intrigue.

By nature, we are similar.
By nurture, we differ greatly.

ANA: XVII, 2

Ancient Chinese peerage was fleeting. Few noble ranks were bestowed in perpetuity, but instead dropped a level with each following generation. A valorous warrior might win himself a dukedom, but his son would be a marquess, his grandson an earl, his great-great-grandson a viscount, and his great-grandson a mere baron. Unless someone in the family performed a new heroic deed, they would fall off the ranks of the nobility after five generations. Such a system encouraged a more active involvement in government and warfare, but could also lead to acts of political desperation. Several generations after the last Shang noble became a peer in the service of the Zhou, his great-grandsons had their post stolen from them by their uncle. One of the two brothers accepted his fate and renounced his inheritance. The other entered into a feud with the uncle, and eventually killed him and was invested as a duke.

It was another crucial moment in the history of Confucius's family, since he was descended from Fuhe, the elder brother who avoided conflict and

5

not the younger one who fought back. From that point, noble rank began to pass through Fuhe's nephews and grand-nephews. Although Fuhe himself was a direct descendant of the penultimate Shang king, he had lost his chance to be a ruler.

Fuhe's descendants were scholars and administrators, all of some renown, but without the high risks and swift rewards of their more belligerent cousins. By 710 BC, the ranks had run out, and Fuhe's great-great-grandson Jia reverted to the status of a commoner. We find him in Chinese sources still serving at the palace as Master of the Horse, but with the mundane surname of Kong.

Despite a reputation for loyalty and uprightness, Jia met with a violent end. An evil minister coveted his beautiful wife, and eventually had him killed. Jia's widow strangled herself with her girdle rather than submit to the murderer, and the tragedy led to a feud between the two families that lasted for several generations.

Tiring of the constant harassment, Jia's great-grandson headed north to the state of Lu, where he and his son both became civil administrators. So it was that, by the sixth century BC, the Kong family had a long reputation for scholarly researches, loyalty, modesty and a refusal to involve themselves in violence. Only one of the Kong family bucked the family trend, and that was Confucius's father, Shuliang He.

Shuliang He was a giant of a man, who had a long military career studded with accolades and dispatches for his strength and bravery. In 562 BC, he was serving as a soldier during a siege, and was one of a squad of attackers who charged through an apparently unguarded gate. The whole thing was a trap arranged by the town's defenders, who planned to drop the heavy portcullis behind the detachment of soldiers, and then massacre them at their leisure within the walls once they had been cut off from their fellow attackers. However, Shuliang He was near the portcullis as it began creaking to a close. Dropping his sword, he grabbed the heavy gate and kept it from reaching the ground, gradually lifting it inch by inch. Seeing the trap, his fellow soldiers were able to beat a fast retreat, while Shuliang He bravely held the portcullis aloft. Only when his comrades had made their escape did he drop the gate and flee himself.

It does not bother me that others do not know me, but it bothers me that I do not know others.

ANA: I, 16

The incident with the portcullis was probably the crowning glory of Shuliang's career. If the dates and

stories match, he was already well into his fifties
when it took place.[4] But as his retirement approached, the brave Shuliang fretted about his family
line. His wife had given him nine daughters and
a son, but the son, Mang-pi, was disabled. Whatever the nature of his disability (and Chinese
sources limit themselves to calling him a 'cripple'),
it left him unable to carry out ancestral rites and
sacrifices. If Shuliang and his forebears were to be
honoured in the afterlife, they would require a more
able heir.[5]

After giving birth to at least ten surviving children, Shuliang's first wife was in no condition to supply another one. The couple had married young, and
her reproductive life was over. Shuliang's only
option was to find a second wife to provide him
with a son, and three nubile candidates were available at the household of the nearby Yan family.

Even refracted through classical Chinese and over
two millennia, Shuliang's meeting with the Yan
daughters comes over as uneasy and tense.[6] The Yan
girls' father reminded his daughters that, although
the man before them was old, he had had a long and
distinguished career. His immediate forebears were
'mere scholars', but father Yan also talked up
Shuliang's distant aristocratic ancestors in the Shang
aristocracy. It would seem that none of this
particularly impressed the Yan girls, who regarded
the tall old man in stony silence.

Eventually, father Yan reminded his daughters
that he was keen on the alliance himself, and asked

them straight who was prepared to accept Shuliang's offer of marriage. The elder girls were wise enough to keep their mouths shut, but the youngest, Zheng-zai, retorted sulkily: 'Why do you ask us, father? It is for you to determine.' That was good enough for father Yan, and he promptly told the girl that she would do – the name *Zheng*-zai can imply someone who is particularly outspoken and argumentative; there is a chance that this was not the first time the girl had answered back.

Be ever mindful of your parents' ages. It may be a source of joy, but it can also be a source of constant concern.

ANA: IV, 21

Shuliang's new wife was many years younger than he, and does not appear to have been popular with her in-laws. One Chinese source even refers to their arrangement as a 'rude coupling'[7] or 'wild union', leading some later commentators to suggest that they were never truly married, though others have claimed the 'wild' part simply refers to the immense difference in their ages.

Details of what happened next are lost, buried amid century after century of writers' attempts to read portent and greatness into Confucius's birth. We only know that Zheng-zai, realising that her husband was not long for the world, prayed desperately for a male child. She also supposedly dreamt that she was visited by the spirits of the five planets, leading a mythical creature known as a *qilin*. Best translated in English as 'unicorn', the appearance of a *qilin* was said to presage the birth or death of a truly momentous individual. Zheng-zai's dream-figures told her that her son would be a 'throneless king', and the befuddled mother-to-be remembered tying an embroidered ribbon around the phantom unicorn's horn. Then she woke up.

Her prayers were answered when she gave birth to a baby boy, in a year generally agreed to be 551 BC. He was called Zhong-ni ('Second Son'), although his mother nicknamed him Qiu, or 'Mound' after a little lump on the top of his head.[8]

Zheng-zai had successfully provided her husband with a male heir, but her troubles were just beginning. When her son was only three years old, the venerable Shuliang passed away and left her a widow. Shuliang was buried at a picturesque location, but neither Zheng-zai nor her infant son appear to have been invited to the funeral.[9]

By all accounts, Confucius grew up in genteel poverty, largely ostracised by Shuliang's first wife and family. However, his early life was not that of a pauper – Confucius did not lack for an education, and was acquainted with the local aristocracy, if not regarded as a member.

By chance or by his mother's design, Confucius grew up obsessed with his reason for entering the world – performing the necessary rites to venerate his father and forebears. Despite the enmity of his relatives, the young Confucius made worship and ritual fundamental parts of his daily routine. Where other children played with toys, the young Confucius reputedly played at religious ceremonies, laying out bowls and plates, and claiming they were sacrificial vessels.

Just as luxury breeds arrogance, so a frugal lifestyle breeds humility. Surely it is better to be humble than to be arrogant.

ANA: VII, 35

True to her wifely duty, his mother also ensured he learnt the songs and hymns of the day, which served as an education of sorts, and possibly the only form of entertainment available during his impoverished upbringing. As an old man, he was once heard saying to children: 'Little ones, why do you not study the songs? For songs will give power to your imagination and heighten your perception, they will bring you friends and teach you irony. When at home, they will bring joy to your parents. When far away, they can bring solace to your prince. Moreover, they will teach you more of birds, beasts, plants and trees.'[10]

What family wealth there may have been must have gone on dowries for his nine sisters, and the continued care of the disabled Mang-pi. The deprivation of Confucius's youth was just enough to give him a healthy obsession with frugality. It also left him with a recognition of the need for knowledge to have useful applications. 'What difference does it make,' he said, 'if a man can sing the three hundred greatest songs, but, when trusted with an official post, does not know how to do his job? If someone is sent away on business, but cannot take control, what difference does it make if he is "educated"? Learning must be of practical use.'[11]

Confucius appeared to have inherited his mother's love of argument, and his father's imposing physique, growing into a towering man, probably over two metres in height.[12] At nineteen years of age, Confucius married a woman from the state of Song, presumably a distant associate of his fallen ancestors. Although the couple carried out their conjugal duties, their relationship was stormy, and Confucius once complained that women, like servants, were impossible to please: 'Show them kindness and they take advantage; keep your distance and they sulk!'[13]

The couple soon produced the first of their three children, and were congratulated by Lu's ruler, the Shining Duke,[14] who presented Confucius with two carp in honour of the occasion. Confucius named the boy Carp after his lord's present, and the poor child was known thereafter by the nickname Top Fish.[15] In years to come, Top Fish was followed by two girls, one who died young and another who lived to adulthood.[16] However, Confucius never seemed to get along with his wife, and some sources report that the couple eventually divorced in their forties.

Matters of depth and importance may be discussed with those who have talent. They should not be debated with those whose talents are mediocre.

ANA: VI, 19

Confucius had attracted the attention of the nobility in other ways. Lu's aristocracy was composed of three branches of the same family, the Shusun, Mengsun and Jisun clans, descended from the three younger children of an earlier ruler.[17] The Jisun clan roused his ire at an early age, when some of its members snubbed him at a banquet by telling him that only gentlemen were permitted entry.[18] He made many comments about the extravagances of the family, whose ostentatious lifestyle was at odds with his frugal existence. He was particularly incensed that the Jisun clan wasted so much wealth on entertainment, while seeming to display little knowledge of the correct protocol for sacrifice and ceremonials. For someone such as Confucius, who had been reared in the knowledge that the performance of certain rituals was his sole reason for existence, the attitude of the Jisun clan was liable, not surprisingly, to cause some frustration.

There are three types of friends that are good for you and three that are bad. You benefit from friendship with those who are upright, loyal and intelligent, but it is harmful to keep the company of flatterers, hypocrites and the ignorant.

ANA: XVI, 4

When he eventually found employment, it was as a civil servant, away from the backbiting and intrigues of the hostile clan. His first posting was as a humble manager in the government grain warehouses. With a wife and young child to support, Confucius threw himself into his work, and diligently kept records of incoming and outgoing stores. It was a boring combination of accountancy and management, with Confucius scratching records on to bamboo strips, and checking to make sure that the grain stores were not under attack from mice or other vermin. 'My calculations must be right,' he said of his job. 'That is all I have to care about.'[19]

It was hardly a glamorous occupation, but someone in a position of authority realised that Confucius was wasted as a warehouse-keeper. Before long he was promoted to a similar supply position, but one involving the management of state herds and flocks. 'The oxen and sheep must be fat and strong,' he commented without relish. 'That is all I have to care about.'[20]

Confucius remained in government positions during his twenties, but his interest in ritual soon paid off in a new posting. In an age with pitifully little literature, and very few people who could read it, learning was primarily transmitted through songs and poetry. Ritual and ceremonial existed primarily to appease and persuade distant gods, but at a secular level, they were designed to educate – even supposedly peripheral elements like statues, paintings, songs of praise, and the music itself were all designed to inform the congregation about the world at large. In being an expert on religious ceremonies and ritual, Confucius was in effect a polymath. If there was anything worth knowing, there was a song about it, and if there was a song about it, Confucius probably knew it. His understanding of songs and poetry was at such an advanced level that he was able to criticise their content and collate variant versions to make a definite canon.[21] This ability eventually secured him a small coterie of students, interested in learning from him the correct way to perform the ceremonies.

One of the first to join Confucius was a brash teenager called Zilu, who boasted to Confucius that his most treasured possession was his long, sharp sword. Confucius replied: 'That, and an education would make you smart.' Zilu retorted that he could cut down a strip of bamboo and sharpen it, turning it into a weapon that would penetrate the hide of a rhino – he demanded to know how education would improve this ability. Confucius pointed out that an intelligent man would have tipped the bamboo with metal and turned it into an arrow, implying that education would hone Zilu in a similar fashion. It was enough to make Zilu become a pupil of the master, though their relationship was often stormy and argumentative, particularly in later years when the nine-year age gap between them would become negligible and they were transformed into a pair of equally grumpy old men.[22]

Zilu and others like him became the first recorded students of Confucius, although the young civil servant's sideline in teaching was put on temporary hold by the death of his mother around 527 BC, leading to the period of prescribed mourning of children for their parents. Since Confucius was only in his early twenties, his mother must have barely been in her forties when she died.[23] 'There are some things I cannot bear to see,' Confucius would say later. 'Narrow-minded men in positions of power, the performance of empty ritual, mourners who do not truly grieve.'[24]

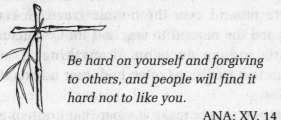

Be hard on yourself and forgiving to others, and people will find it hard not to like you.

ANA: XV, 14

The length of the mourning period was twenty-seven months, spreading across three calendar years, symbolic of the time that parents spent rearing a child until it was able to walk for itself. For the 'false mourners' Confucius derided, it would be glossed over as quickly as possible with a few perfunctory ceremonies, and possibly some half-hearted fasting. Others, in search of an excuse for a prolonged mid-career vacation, would take the full mourning period, but use it as an excuse to avoid their duties.

But the death of the mother who had raised him single-handedly was not regarded so flippantly by Confucius. She had reared him as a master of ritual, and he performed the mourning ceremonies for her with the utmost adherence to detail.

He also took great pains to arrange not only for her funeral, but also to track down the site of his father's burial, exhume his father's and mother's coffins, and eventually lay the couple to rest side by side at a new gravesite. Although Confucius normally kept strictly to protocol, he broke with tradition by erecting an earth mound over the double grave. Heavy rainfall caused the mound to sag, and for Confucius to regret his sudden decision. If anything, it reminded him that traditions often had their origins in practicalities.

Asides in one source make it clear that Confucius already had several disciples by the time of his mother's death, as he delegated some of the funeral arrangements to them. It was they who observed the collapse of his mother's grave mound, and reported it to Confucius, who listened in stunned silence. Sobbing, the master eventually responded: 'They don't make graves like they used to.'[25]

Even though he had pupils of his own, Confucius continued his studies. With communications slow and sluggish between population centres, he took every available opportunity to learn from visitors from afar. In autumn 525 BC, the state received a royal visitor from a distant and puny kingdom, whose court was responsible for making sacrifices to one of the region's earliest rulers. Confucius listened intently as the dignitary expounded on the royal line of early China, and stayed long after the welcoming banquet was supposed to end, quizzing the visitor about the way in which his own country conducted rites and worship.[26]

He also conducted advanced studies in music with the chief bard of the court, since he regarded mastery of music as a metaphor for the growth of an individual. In the early stages, the would-be musician must be disciplined like a child. Only when he has mastered the basics is he freer to improvise. 'Music can be learned,' said Confucius.

'At first, discipline must be strict, all parts sounding together, but as the musicians develop, they gain more liberty to improvise. The tones remain pure and consistent, until the end, in several harmonies.'[27]

As he approached his thirties, he regarded his own skills as having risen above the basic. He knew the intimate details not only of his own state's protocol, but of the ceremonies of other states. His quest for knowledge had started to pay off, as the attendance of Confucius at treaty negotiations or a diplomatic mission would ensure that his countrymen would do nothing to make the foreign negotiators feel ill at ease. Instead, he was able to present the actions of his compatriots in a permanently positive light. Visitors would see the people of Lu conducting perfect religious ceremonies. Songs and entertainments would not offend the sensibilities of guests from afar. Sacrifices were well chosen, as were the interpretations of the royal diviners. Confucius was able to ensure that official events ran smoothly, and such a talent was extremely useful in an age when meetings were often held between armed warriors with battalions of soldiers ready to strike at a word. The tall, quiet civil servant's devotion to learning had turned him into a valuable member of the court.

2

Scholar and Teacher

At thirty I stood on my own two feet. *ANA*: II, 3

Unknown to Confucius, his voracious interest in education and his family's long-standing aversion to power-struggles had reached the notice of the state's chief minister, Meng-xi. On his deathbed, Meng-xi told his successor that Confucius was wise indeed – whether he meant in general or in his avoidance of political intrigue is unclear. Whatever Meng-xi's motives, his advice did not go unheeded. After his death, his successor soon approached Confucius in search of further education, either out of genuine respect for his aptitude, or perhaps simply because the impoverished scholar did not seem to present much of a threat.[1] As he entered his thirties, Confucius finally found himself rewarded for his years of intense studies, not with a government post, but with a stipend as a professional scholar and teacher – two of Meng-xi's sons became his students. The ruling class of Lu were prepared to pay Confucius to teach them what he had learned, and to fund further acquisition of knowledge with a research allowance. In return, Confucius appears to have served as an occasional adviser to the state's ruler, a man known to posterity as the Shining Duke.

Search ten houses, and you are bound to find someone as honest and loyal as I, but I doubt if you could find someone who shares my love of learning.

ANA: V, 27

Confucius was determined to put his grant-maintained status to good use, and soon put in a request to travel out of his home state to the distant capital, Luoyang. He asked for state assistance, and was given a chariot and two horses for his trip. By the standards of the day it was an immense distance – over 200 miles, through at least two other feudal territories, whose alliances with Lu could not always be guaranteed. Confucius did not travel alone, but in the company of several disciples, and possibly with other members of the Lu court on diplomatic or trade missions.[2]

Luoyang was the religious centre of the Chinese world. Here, the ruling kings of China were responsible for the greatest and purest of rituals to the most high-ranking of spirits. Although the secular power of the kings had waned beyond repair, they still exerted great religious authority. Confucius took considerable interest in the rituals of the capital, in order to make the ceremonies of Lu as much like those of Luoyang as possible. He inspected the outdoor area where sacrifices were made to Heaven and Earth, measuring the grounds and observing the behaviour of royal officials. He also visited the Hall of Light where the kings would receive foreign visitors; there to check its *feng shui* – the nature of the building, its placement, and its interior design. In Confucius's day, a building's ruling direction, its entrance-ways and architecture were a vital component of political power in the human realm. From Confucius's later comments on religion, we can guess that he was less interested in the magic of kingship than in the way in which outside visitors were treated. Just as Christian churches in the Middle Ages sought to educate visitors with their windows and statuary, the halls of the kings established their authority through decoration.[3] The walls of the Hall of Light were decorated with images of China's ancient kings reaching back into times of legend, each with accompanying notices on their vices and virtues. Nobody entering the hall could avoid gazing at several parables of past kingship, or indeed the most recent picture on the walls, which showed the previous ruler with the current king as an infant on his knee. 'Here you see how the Zhou dynasty became so great', Confucius said. 'As we use a glass to examine the forms of things, so must we study antiquity in order to understand the present.'[4]

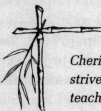

Cherish your old knowledge, and strive for new, that you may be a teacher of others.

ANA: II, 11

Confucius also inspected the ancestral temple of the royal family, which he regarded as an equally important part of state architecture. He was not disappointed. Just as the portraits in the Hall of Light implied respect and remembrance, the ancestral temple carried that idea into the afterlife. Remembering the words and deeds of ancestors was of crucial value to Confucius, who lived in a time when so much knowledge was lost by each generation, only to be discovered anew, passed on by word of mouth, and then lost once more. He was even more impressed by a statue in the temple that made a bold statement about respecting one's rulers. Crafted from bronze, it depicted a man whose mouth was held shut by three clasps. On his back was written a brief epigram about the virtues of silence. 'Observe it, my children', he said to his followers. 'These words are true.'[5]

Confucius himself caused a stir at the capital, and dazzled some of the local ministers with his wit and decorum. 'When he speaks, he praises the ancient kings,' said an approving court musician. 'He moves along the path of humility and courtesy. He has heard of every subject, and retains it with a strong memory. His knowledge of things seems inexhaustible. Have we not in him the rising of a sage?'[6]

For Confucius, the highlight of his visit was his meeting with the curator of the royal libraries, Li Er. The aged Li Er was perhaps the only person in China with a better grasp of ceremonies than the young Confucius, and the two men supposedly enjoyed a long meeting. Li Er, however, was not quite the mentor that Confucius was expecting. In fact, he was growing increasingly disenchanted with courtly life, and was already planning his resignation and retirement. Although we remember Confucius as an old man, it is easy to forget that he was once young, too, and Li Er's words to him show signs of an older teacher reining in the youthful excesses of a pupil. Li Er thought there was little point in alluding to the successes of old, when modern states refused to learn from their examples. He sternly warned the young Confucius that a political life was fraught with disappointments, and that success in his chosen career would only lead to enemies in high places. 'Those whom you talk about are dead', he said, 'and their bones are mouldered to dust. Only their words remain. When the superior man gets his time, he mounts aloft; but when the time is against him, he moves as if his feet were entangled . . . Put away your proud air and many desires, your insinuating habit and wild will.'

Before long, Li Er's admonishments made themselves felt in a new twist to Confucius's own personal philosophy. He displayed little interest in the afterlife or the spirit world, instead concentrating on protocol in the here and now. Rituals served an educational purpose for Confucius, but he did not care for discussion of whether or not they could bring divine aid.

It is possible that Confucius's eternal sparring partner Zilu noticed this change in attitude, since he pointedly asked him about duties he had towards the spirit world. 'We cannot serve the dead', Confucius replied, 'until we have served the living . . . First know what life is, before seeking to know death.'[7]

Over the course of his life, Confucius would allude on several occasions to things he had learned from Li Er. He also reportedly compared the librarian to a dragon, soaring high above mundane creatures, and immune to everyday distractions. He praised Li Er, not only for his wisdom, but for his policy of setting a good example for others. 'Good people must honour virtue and bring enlightenment to others', Confucius said. 'Dragons and sages are not the only beings with the potential to know all and endure hardship. Be kind to those below you, let them observe your example like the markings of a Dragon – after seeing such a creature, few would forget the experience.'[8]

Li Er, however, did not remain in the capital long after Confucius's return to Lu. Instead, the librarian resigned his post and became a hermit. Referred to as *Lao Zi*, or the 'Old Master', he eventually disappeared, leaving only his writings in the *Dao De Jing*, the holy scripture of Daoism.

There are people who act without understanding their reasons, but I am not one of them. Hear all evidence, then select what is worthy, then follow that. See much and remember.

ANA: VII, 27

Confucius returned safely to Lu, and no doubt hoped to continue his state-funded acquisition of knowledge. However, the country was soon torn apart by a quarrel between its three most powerful families, and Confucius was no longer safe.

Nothing demonstrates the political instability of the time more keenly than the source of Confucius's undoing. According to the *Records of the Historian*, civil strife in the state of Lu escalated over a silly little incident. An argument got out of hand at a cockfight between birds owned by rival noblemen. One of the noblemen somehow managed to insult the Shining Duke himself, leading the ageing ruler to order the arrest of the offender. Needless to say, the rebellious nobleman was one of Confucius's old tormenters, the Jisun clan.

> *The virtuous always speak correctly, but merely saying the right thing is no proof of virtue. Heroes may be brave, but not all of those who act bravely are necessarily heroes.*
>
> ANA: XIV, 5

The quarrel masked other tensions. As the Shining Duke's reign drifted into its twilight years, nobles in rival families saw their chance to make a grab for power. Some demonstration that the Duke had lost his mandate to rule might be all that it took to get rid of him and his untested heir.

In turn, the Duke could not permit any insult to go unpunished. Although the fight may have begun over a sporting event, it soon grew into a contest over the state itself. When the offender resisted arrest, the Duke's army marched in to apprehend him, to discover that many other nobles were prepared to back the rebel. Two rival houses backed the contender, and, in the skirmish that followed, the Duke's forces were defeated. After reigning for twenty-five years, the Shining Duke was forced to flee the territory he once ruled, running north to seek asylum in the neighbouring state of Qi.

Almost overnight, Lu became unsafe for Confucius, whose association with the defeated Duke stretched back many years. With extreme reluctance, he followed his patron to Qi, hoping that his sojourn there would be short – with a common border, the people of Qi and Lu had long been intermittent enemies.

Confucius seems to have had mixed feelings about the quality of life in Qi – his comments contain both words of high praise and embittered attacks. Such a bipolar attitude is best explained through the stress of his exile; with his homeland suddenly closed to him, he was forced to marshal contradictory attitudes to his new abode. In the course of his short stay in Qi, he tried to make the best of his compulsory visit, only to face growing disappointment.

Nevertheless, a swift journey to Qi was Confucius's best option, and he set out with several of his disciples. There was safety in numbers, particularly with the belligerent Zilu as one of the party – a group of healthy young armed men was unlikely to attract trouble from all but the largest of bandit groups. Confucius rode in a carriage, presumably accompanied by others of his group on foot or in chariots of their own.[9]

A wall separated Qi from Lu, but the borderland was lawless. As Confucius and his entourage passed Mount Tai, which marked the general border, they came upon a woman weeping by a graveside. The group seems to have initially paid little attention, but her grief did not let up. Eventually Confucius called a halt to the journey, sending Zilu over to ask her what was wrong. 'You weep', Zilu said to her, 'as if you have experienced sorrow upon sorrow.'

'It is so', she replied. 'My father-in-law was killed here by a tiger, and my husband also; and now my son has met the same fate.'

It was certainly a sob-story of some weight, but Confucius, ever the practically minded, asked the woman if she had perhaps considered moving to somewhere less dangerous. 'There is no tyranny here', she replied simply, much to Confucius's astonishment.

'My children', said Confucius to his followers. 'Mark this well, oppressive government is fiercer than a tiger.'[10]

Borders in ancient China were often not clearly defined. In areas without a river or coastline to mark territory clearly, the lands of one ruler gradually melted into those of another. Confucius and his followers had encountered the weeping woman at the point where the authority of Lu petered out and eventually yielded to the sphere of influence of Qi. They had passed through the region of greatest danger, and made it through unscathed.[11]

Ignoring someone worthy of hearing is an insult to them. speaking to someone unworthy of hearing is an insult to yourself. The truly wise neither lose companions, nor waste their words.

ANA: XV, 7

Supposedly, Confucius was soon able to tell that they had entered a civilised area. The carriage and outriders pressed on, past peasants working in fields, and villagers dealing with their daily chores. Confucius was impressed even with the way they walked, commenting to his driver that the boy carrying a pitcher seemed to have internalised many of the teachings of the sages' music. No extant classical Chinese song records the virtues of correct posture, but presumably Confucius was impressed either with the boy's mode of lifting, or simply a gait that reflected regular dancing exercise.

Confucius was ready to be impressed with the standard of learning in Qi. On arrival, he commented that he did not believe music could be so excellent.[12] By an accident of preservation, the court musicians of Qi possessed the purest versions of the original music of the Zhou dynasty. Confucius realised that the music played in Qi ceremonies was the closest possible match to the saintly originals of olden times, ungarbled by copying errors or later interpolations. He threw himself into studies and conferences with Qi scholars, and was welcomed by the local aristocracy.

The disciple Yuan Si became an important official, but when Confucius offered him nine hundred measures of grain, he refused. Confucius said: 'Do not refuse. Take them, and give them away amongst the villagers.

ANA: VI, 3, iii

Qi's ruler, the Honoured Duke,[13] had met Confucius several years earlier, when the Duke visited Lu on state business. The pair had discussed politics, carefully avoiding unwitting insults or slights by keeping to matters of ancient history. Confucius had praised the act of a legendary king, who once freed a slave and made him a powerful minister.[14] He meant to imply that the Duke should practise a meritocracy, promoting those who were competent in their jobs, and not alienating talented ministers through favouritism. The Duke was impressed with Confucius's words, which is more than can be said for his chief minister Yan Ying, who was also in attendance. Whether or not Confucius intended his words to be a veiled insult, Yan Ying saw it as such.

Some years later, when Confucius arrived in Qi and hoped to presume on his earlier meeting with the Honoured Duke, Yan Ying had not forgotten their first encounter. Undoubtedly, he regarded Confucius as a threat, and seethed while the Duke welcomed his new guest[15] over the course of several discussions on statecraft and politics. Before long, the Duke offered Confucius a permanent post, suggesting that he might like to be given authority over a town. Confucius, however, found a way of declining the offer – although he had publicly praised the standard of learning in Qi, in private he seemed less positive. 'A gentleman only receives rewards for services rendered', he confided to his followers. 'I have given advice to the Honoured Duke, but he has yet to follow it. And now he wants to confer this title upon me? He is very far from understanding me!'[16]

Conceivably, Confucius would have been more willing to stay in Qi if the Duke were prepared to carry out some of his advice, but none of his suggestions took hold. The Duke's initial agreement soon met with resistance further down the chain of command, as his ministers and officers invented obstacles and counter-arguments to discredit the newcomer. Paramount among the resentful opposition, of course, was chief minister Yan Ying. While Yan Ying struggled with the practicalities of running the state, and worried over the implications of the civil strife over the border in the state of Lu, his lord and master idled the days away discussing matters of mere theory with the new arrival.

Yan Ying and Confucius became open rivals – implicit in many of Confucius's dialogues with the Duke was his opinion that the Duke was being let down by his ministers. Ironically, Yan Ying might not have been the minister at fault. He and Confucius seem to have had more in common than otherwise. Both were proud, well-educated men of sterling ability, and classical sources appear strangely contradictory about Confucius's time in Qi. Confucius's own reaction to life in Qi seems schizophrenic – he praises the quality of Qi's ceremonies, but pours scorn on its ministers. He jockeys for a position as an adviser to Qi's ruler, although in private he complains that the Honoured Duke never listens, and does not command the respect of his people. Most crucially, he embarks on a feud with the man in Qi's government who seems most like himself, butting heads and egos over matters of state, when cooperation between the two scholars might have solved many of Qi's problems.

A surviving account from the *Kong Family Masters' Anthology* shows Confucius managing to answer his host back and insult a superior minister in the space of a single conversation – hardly the diplomatic tact he was to show in later life. When a minister arrived late for a meeting, he offered as an excuse the fact that he had been obliged to defend an accused man from persecution by a local dignitary. The Honoured Duke was impressed, and boasted to Confucius that his officers were virtuous men – for even the prosecutor had been prepared to listen to a case for the defence.

The disciple Yuan Si became an important official, but when Confucius offered him nine hundred measures of grain, he refused. Confucius said: 'Do not refuse. Take them, and give them away amongst the villagers.'

ANA: VI, 3, iii

Confucius, however, managed to marshal a reply that put everyone in their place. He pointed out that a truly virtuous official would have hired decent employees from the start, thereby ensuring that he did not waste any time on unnecessary legal proceedings. 'I spoke too soon', said the Honoured Duke, suitably chastened. 'But had I not, how would I have heard the Master's teachings?'[17] Considering that Confucius had managed to belittle him, the late-arriving official, and the minister who prosecuted the case, it was a remarkably gracious response.

There is nothing I can do about those who do not think before they act.

ANA: XV, 15

It was not the only time that Confucius risked overstepping the mark in his dialogues with the Honoured Duke. The Duke, who was considering passing over his eldest son in the succession, once asked Confucius how a government should best be run. In his answer, Confucius took the opportunity to register his disapproval once more. 'There is government', he said, 'when the prince is a prince, and the minister is a minister; when the father is a father and the son is a son.'[18] In the view of Confucius, the Duke was wrong to ignore the protocols of succession, and his ministers were wrong to increase their authority beyond that defined in their job titles.

Keeping things hypothetical, the Duke asked Confucius what would happen, say, in a state where such protocols were not rigidly observed. He wondered aloud if such a state would have the outward appearance of prosperity, but already be subject to rot within. Possibly, the Duke mused, officers would continue to collect taxes, and the government warehouses would still have an income of grain, but ultimately, corruption elsewhere would lead to waste. 'Even if I have my grain,' the Duke wondered, 'will I be able to eat it?' The *Analects*, where this story comes from, does not record Confucius's reply. Perhaps he realised that it was best to say nothing, and left the Duke to wonder for himself which ministers would be best replaced.

The Duke never considered firing Yan Ying, but was certainly pleased enough with Confucius's replies to try him out in a government position. Perhaps noting Confucius's former work experience in the state of Lu, the Duke suggested that the new arrival could be put to work managing one of Qi's feudal sub-districts.

However, this was Yan Ying's chance to fight back, and he did so with a long series of reasons why Confucius was not suitable for the task. Chief among his excuses was Confucius's relative lack of experience. It was all very well, Yan Ying argued, for Confucius to pontificate about ancient kings and ideal government, but platitudes about frugal living and just behaviour were of little use in the real world. 'These scholars are impractical', he said, 'and cannot be imitated.'

Without dedication, none shall respect you and your studies will suffer. Value faithfulness and sincerity above all other things. Have no friends who are not equal to yourself. When you make a mistake, do not be afraid to make amends.

ANA: I, 8

Far from being a worthy candidate for promotion and service, Yan Ying saw Confucius as a disaster waiting to happen – an airy academic whose adherence to ceremonial would be a drain on more important funds. People like Confucius, Yan Ying argued, were 'haughty and conceited in their own views, so that they will not be content in inferior positions. They set a high value on all funeral ceremonies, give way to their grief, and will waste their property on great burials, so that they would only be injurious to the common manners.'[19] Yan Ying finished his character assassination with a reminder that Confucius dealt in abstract theory, while practice was another matter. 'Confucius lays such stress on appearance and costume, elaborate etiquette and codes of behaviour, that it would take generations to learn his rules', he said. 'One lifetime would not be enough! To adopt his way of reforming the state would not be putting the common people first.'[20]

Yan Ying's hatchet job had a remarkable effect on his ruler. Not only did the Duke set aside his plans to offer Confucius a government post, but he also began to regard the visitor with a certain icy detachment. The next time they were both at a public occasion, instead of chatting amicably with Confucius about ceremonial matters, the Duke simply ignored him.

The honeymoon period over, Confucius found other courtiers less friendly, too. At some point, it was made known to the Duke that, in terms of the strict courtly propriety about which Confucius so often made such a fuss, Confucius was being treated in a manner in excess of his actual station. He was a servant of a ruler in exile, and hence in a state of career limbo – neither truly possessing his original rank, nor actually bestowed with one of equivalent local worth. It was simply not becoming for the Duke to treat him as if he were a visiting dignitary. Instead, his status was discreetly demoted a rank or two, which in turn placed limits on his access to the Duke.

Before long, the Honoured Duke was heard saying that he was 'too old' to put Confucius's advice into practice. 'I cannot make use of his doctrines,' said the Honoured Duke eventually, bringing Confucius's unofficial probationary period to an abrupt end. The Duke, Confucius noted sourly in later years, 'had a thousand teams, each of four horses, but on the day of his death, the people did not praise him for a single virtue.'[21]

Confucius saw that he had no future in the state of Qi. Although the former ruler of Lu would remain there in exile till the end of his days, the Qi court-iers had made it abundantly clear that Confucius was not welcome. No longer appreciated at court, he could only expect an increasingly frosty reception as time wore on. It was time for him to leave, and with conflict fomenting to the west, his only option was to head south again, back to the state of Lu, where his own strict rules of propriety would preclude him from accepting employment with the squabbling ruling families. Still in his mid-thirties, Confucius was effectively unemployed and unem-ployable. Nevertheless, he made preparations to return to Lu. 'There are three errors you must avoid in the presence of the honourable and high-ranking', a much older and wiser Confucius would say. 'If you speak out of turn, you are behaving rashly. If you do not speak when you should, you are behaving deceitfully. But if you speak without first observing the mood of your superior, you are behaving blindly.'[22]

There is an apocryphal story in the *Kong Family Masters' Anthology* that claims Yan Ying had a change of heart. Confucius's long-standing rival came to see him while he was holding a banquet at his lodgings, and waited until all the other diners had left. When they were alone, he told Confucius that despite all he had said, the state of Qi needed men like him. He begged him not to leave the country, telling him that the state was in danger, its government like the driver of a runaway chariot, pelting headlong towards a deep precipice.

> *Learning is like building. If I am making an earth mound, and advance a single bucket at a time, what matters is that I am advancing. But if I stop one bucket away from completion, what matters is that I have stopped.*
>
> ANA: IX, 18

Confucius, however, had set his heart on leaving. He told Yan Ying that it was already too late, not necessarily for the state of Qi, but for the ruling clique of which Yan Ying was a part. Confucius was quite sure that the Duke would enjoy a successful reign, and did not doubt for a moment that Yan Ying would live out his days in his post, but he expected their heirs would swiftly be supplanted by a rival clan. Throwing Yan Ying's chariot analogy back in his face, Confucius told him that he doubted that he could return the state to its true course, even if he was prepared to get out and push.[23]

With that, Confucius left the state of Qi behind – returning from physical exile, but with his political career in tatters.

3

Editor and Recluse

At forty I had no doubts. *ANA*: II, 3

Confucius was aghast at what he found back home
in the state of Lu. With the Shining Duke absent, the
three most powerful families had happily divided
up the territory between them. Since they could
already do as they pleased, they made no attempt to
make their usurpation official. They possessed a
sufficient quantity of troops and officers to run the
country to their satisfaction, and the feeble royal
domain made no attempt to intercede on behalf of
the exiled Duke.

Paramount among the victors was the hated Jisun
clan, with whom Confucius had crossed paths as a
young man. Contemporary sources give little idea as
to whether life under the clan and their cronies was
better or worse than it had been under the Shining
Duke, but presumably it was bearable for much of
the population. There was certainly no revolt on the
part of the peasant population; life for many in Lu

went on as before, but Confucius was scandalised at the liberties taken by the *de facto* rulers.

As usual, Confucius regarded ritual as the cornerstone of all human activity. In his idea of the perfect world, the right king was in charge, and ruled over a class of 'nobles' that truly warranted the name. Among the tasks of this upper class, in addition to management and logistics, there would, of course, be a number of important ceremonial functions, in order to ensure Heaven remained appeased, and everything in nature remained in its proper place.

There is more to ritual than gifts of jade and silk. There is more to music than mere bells and drums.

ANA: XVII, 11

The situation in Lu could not be further from this ideal. The state's appointed ruler remained in exile, while the nobles who had defied him ruled as they saw fit. And the Jisun clan did not set much stock in mere rituals. They picked and chose from the available ceremonies, and could not care less whether they got things right by Confucius's strict rules.

The *Analects* reports Confucius spluttering with indignation at the behaviour of the Jisun clan. One ceremony involved a number of officiator-priests in a hall, whose job was to keep time during the service. Sometimes translated as 'dancers' or 'panto-mimes', these officers would clap, chant or perform a series of ritual steps that both venerated the gods and also permitted the chief priest to time his own ritualised movements with care. The number of dancers in a ceremony varied with the rank of the attendant noble – a great minister might expect four rows, for example. In the days of the Shining Duke, the correct protocol would require six rows, a number that would also suffice for anyone of princely rank. But under the Jisun clan, the Lu temple precinct had *eight* rows of dancers, an extravagant spectacle truly worthy of only a king. 'If he'll put up with this,' commented Confucius of the clan's ruler, 'he'll put up with anything!'[1]

Insult was added to injury by the choice of song at the ceremony. As Confucius listened in astonishment, the worshippers began a particular hymn that heralded the clearing away of the sacrificial vessels. The lyrics referred quite distinctly to the presence of princes as high priests, while 'the king himself sat gravely on the throne'. And yet the true king was hundreds of miles away, and there was not a prince in sight; such a travesty was an affront against Heaven. To a ritual specialist like Confucius it was an absolute disaster, inviting divine disapproval, and who knows what else – fire, flood, famine, anything was possible while the Jisun clan were in charge.[2]

To some, Confucius's indignation may sound insufferably pedantic – in fact, he was regarded as such by a fair number of his contemporaries. But his obsession with ceremony was his way of pointing out a general malaise. As he saw it, if the Jisun clan were prepared to behave in such an ignorant and cavalier manner towards religious ceremonies, what other liberties were they taking with their duties to Heaven?[3] Were the granaries being kept stocked in case of famine? Were the taxes being collected and the borders maintained? In an age of slow communication, the only clue Confucius had lay in the behaviour of the land's rulers, and he found them wanting.

He also suspected, rightly, that extravagances like extra lines of temple dancers were eating into funds better retained for more practical uses. One minister in the service of the clan reputedly squandered vast sums cossetting his pets. 'He kept a large tortoise in a little house,' Confucius pointed out, 'with little hills on top of the pillars, and representations of duckweed! Where is the wisdom in that?'[4]

Some disciples, sympathetic to the group that would soon represent their sole chance of local employment, tried to remind Confucius that not all the clan members were completely bad. Some, they argued, even behaved occasionally in a manner of which Confucius might approve, such as another state officer who famously thought each decision over three times before acting. 'Twice would have been enough,' grumbled Confucius, still convinced of the clan's fecklessness.[5]

Accordingly, Confucius desired no part of Lu's new government, although it is likely that Lu's government wanted nothing to do with him, either. 'Your time has passed if you are despised at forty', Confucius said,[6] and sought the company of those who did not hold him in contempt.

If you treat those below you with
disdain, you will be in danger.
For the true of heart to remain
righteous is like climbing a tree.
The higher you ascend, the greater
the distance you may fall.

SDA, 5

Confucius went into retirement, and busied himself with his growing coterie of students, and with an extensive survey of literature. He hoped for better things, and spent fifteen years as a teacher. Meanwhile, at the court itself, the usurpers reaped as they had sown, and soon found themselves barely able to control a civil service of unruly ministers. The ruler who would 'put up with anything' was eventually forced to put up with blackmail and imprisonment by one of his more powerful and corrupt ministers.

After such a meteoric rise to prominence during the rule of the Shining Duke, Confucius's absence from the court did not go unnoticed. He was even asked why he did not involve himself in the running of the state.

Do not impose on your ruler, and, moreover, if you must disagree, do so to his face.

ANA: XIV, 23

He replied: 'I am a loyal son; I am a dutiful brother. These qualities are part of the running of the state. I am already part of the government, why should there be more?'[7] His words were an allusion to the *Book of History*, but they are often quoted as if they were his own, since they seem to contain so much of his essential attitude. He venerated his dead parents, he cared for his disabled brother, and he tried to lead by example, hoping that if everyone did as he did, the troubles of the world would cease. One of the central tenets of Confucianism, lasting for two millennia since the time of the Master himself, has been that everyone has duties according to their rank and immediate responsibilities, and that if they are all carried out suitably, then the bigger issues resolve themselves. 'Never let your faith falter,' he said to his disciples. 'Love learning. If attacked, be ready to die for truth. Do not enter a place of danger, nor a state in revolt. When justice prevails under Heaven, then show yourself. When it does not, then hide your face. When government is good, be ashamed of poverty and deprivation. When government is bad, be ashamed of riches and honour.'[8]

The *Analects* gives us several glimpses of the lively debates that went on in Confucian classes. Posterity has given us Confucian sayings handed down as if they had sprung fully formed from the Master's brain, but many of his conclusions were tested, honed and refined over years of seminars and debates. Confucius encouraged deduction and argument in his academy – students were expected to defer to their teachers, but also to speak up when they had questions. All Confucius demanded of his charges was that they be willing to learn. 'There is no point in teaching those who do not wish to learn,' he said, 'nor in helping those who do not ask for it. If I present one corner of a subject, and my students cannot deduce the other three, I do not repeat my lesson.'[9]

Money was no object, either, and Confucius accepted students from all backgrounds, regardless of wealth or social status. 'If someone were to bring me a bundle of dried meat as payment, I would still not refuse to instruct them', he said.[10] While his successors in later ages were often accused of snobbery and exclusionism, Confucius himself only operated on the basis of available facts. He accepted one pupil, Zichang, even though the youth had previously served time in jail. Rather than stigmatise Zichang for his past transgressions, Confucius welcomed him into the seminars and discussions, and eventually pronounced him one of his star pupils. He was sufficiently impressed with him to go one step further, and granted him his own daughter's hand in marriage.[11]

A gentleman would rescue a man trapped in a well, but he would not jump in himself. He is not perfect, but he is not stupid, either.

ANA: VI, 24

Later generations would paint an idyllic picture of the Confucian academy, with neatly dressed scholars wandering leafy precincts discussing matters of philosophy. However, the classes often took a more boisterous tone, and the *Analects* recounts several incidents when Confucius lost his patience with slow or unruly audiences. At all times, however, he still retained his caustic wit.

One pupil, Ran Qiu, dared to excuse himself with a crack about his own idleness. 'It is not that I do not like your teachings', he said. 'Just that I do not have the energy to follow them.'

Confucius, however, was cutting in his reply. 'If it were down to energy, you could rest halfway', he said. 'But you have not even taken the first step.'[12]

'No one heeds my teachings,' he once complained to his class in exasperation. 'I might as well get on to a raft and drift off to sea, accompanied by a disciple. Probably Zilu.' On hearing this, Zilu was exceedingly happy – the older scholar was clearly smirking on the sidelines on that day. 'For Zilu', continued Confucius, 'is the only one foolish enough to follow me.'[13]

The period is also the likely setting for the only sizeable incident reported in the life of Confucius's son Top Fish. Growing up with a father whose sole income stemmed from teaching, Top Fish became an indifferent student at Confucius's impromptu academy. As his teens gave way to his twenties, the boy remained one of his father's followers, although presumably finances were so tight that he had little other option.

As Confucius's followers grew in number, a divide began to appear between the generations. Long-term disciples such as Zilu often appeared to be closer in age to Confucius than to their fellow students, and the natural rules of propriety dictated that the younger disciples should defer to the older ones in all matters. Some of the new arrivals, however, suspected that there might be a secret 'inner knowledge' reserved for Confucius's closest confidants, and hoped to find out for themselves what they were supposedly missing in class. Their searches, however, were to prove fruitless – hoarding knowledge for himself went against Confucius's personal ethics of education.

Nevertheless, the disciple Chen Kang approached Top Fish and asked if his father had ever given him any secret teaching. 'No,' Top Fish replied, 'though once I passed my father in the courtyard, and he said: "Have you studied the *Book of Songs*?" When I said no, he said: "If you do not study the *Songs*, you will have nothing worth talking about." I immediately began studying the *Book of Songs*, but when I passed him again, he asked if I had studied the *Book of Rites*. When I said no, he said: "If you do not study the *Rites*, you will have no character." These are the only private instructions I have received from my father.'

Chen Kang was very pleased. 'I asked one question, but received three answers,' he boasted. 'I have heard of the importance of the *Songs*, of the *Rites*, and also that a true gentleman has no secrets, not even to share with his son.'[14]

Confucius had long been held in high esteem as a scholar, even by those who had little time for his researches or his advice. His long period of political inactivity allowed him to refine his knowledge to truly unprecedented levels. Fifteen years of private reading and public seminars gave him an unparalleled insight into the literature of his day. To modern eyes, such an accomplishment sounds little different from any other career in academia, but 500 years before the birth of Christ Confucius was one of the first individuals ever to live such a life. Formerly, noble families had appointed tutors for their children by finding specialists and paying them to give occasional lessons. In making study itself his life's work Confucius became the first true academic.[15]

> *Who here does not have the strength to do nothing but good for a whole day? It is possible for everyone.*
>
> ANA: IV, 6

In an age of few books, he also set about compiling approved editions from the material that was available. His question to Top Fish about the study of the *Songs* referred to one of several extant books that he was said to have edited – a distillation of thousands of popular ballads into 300 acknowledged classics. The *Analects* contains a couple of moments from what could have been the first editorial conferences in history, as Confucius argued about song lyrics. 'If I must take a single phrase to summarise the three hundred great songs,' Confucius said, 'then it is – *Let there be no evil in your thoughts*. If people are controlled by laws, and kept in line by punishments, they will merely try to avoid the punishment, but will have no sense of guilt. If people are led by good example, and guided by a sense of propriety, they will have a sense of right and wrong, but be encouraged to be good.'[16]

Be courteous, and you will not be humiliated. Be wide-ranging, and you will gain the love of the people. Be honourable, and others shall trust you. Be diligent, and you shall eventually succeed in every task.
ANA: XVII, 6

A stickler as ever for correctness in all things, Confucius did his best to ensure that no substandard song survived in his approved repertoire. If the songs did not inform or encourage the best way to live in harmony with others, he censored them from his collection. He is even reported to have rejected some on grounds of bad metaphors or illogical analogies. Confucius rejected a song that went: 'The flowers of the cherry tree, Sway to and fro upon the branch, It's not that I do not miss my love, But her home is far, far away.' Confucius said: 'He does not miss her. What would a true lover care about distance?'[17] When educating the masses required a small but wide-ranging number of hymns and songs, there was no space in Confucius's compilation for bad grammar or muddy phrasing.

Confucius did not merely work on the the *Book of Songs* during this period. He also edited the *Book of History*, *Book of Rites* and *Book of Music*, fixing centuries of tradition in the best possible forms.[18] His students were expected to know of the great deeds of the kings of old, the ceremonies that kept the universe in balance, and the songs and music that should be played at them, and by compiling all available materials, Confucius put his personal stamp of approval on much earlier tradition.

These books formed the core of his curriculum, and were taught to many hundreds of students, although only a few became full 'graduates' of the school, deemed proficient in all areas. While the Jisun clan continued to fly in the face of propriety, their rule oversaw the creation of a generation of scholars able to tell them exactly where they were going wrong.

However, the clan was not in a mood to listen. In 510 BC, the Shining Duke finally died in exile, an event which was, ironically, to prove far more damaging to the Jisun clan than attacking them with an army. With their nominal ruler now dead, they were obliged to mount ceremonies in his honour and also to appoint his son as their new leader. However briefly hopes may have been raised, they were soon dashed as the clans continued to ride roughshod over tradition. The Duke's son was passed over in the succession, and instead the clan selected the Shining Duke's brother as their new ruler. He was known to posterity as the Decisive Duke, and his epitaph would eventually read: 'Greatly anxious, pacifier of the people.'[19]

By this point, several of Confucius's disciples were graduating from the academy and finding government jobs, both within the state of Lu and beyond. After years in the political wilderness, his absence from court life was clearly getting to him at last. Earlier critics still stung him with their accusations that he knew only theory and nothing of practice. As he entered middle age, he had yet to prove that any of his ideas would actually improve the running of a state, although some of his disciples were finding fame by applying his teachings elsewhere.

Confucius still refused to serve the incumbent administration, citing the continued infringements of the Jisun clan as his reason. The two government officials whom Confucius most despised were Yang Hu[20] and Gongshan Furao, although the feeling does not appear to have been mutual. While Confucius busied himself with his scholars, these leading Lu officers made several attempts to offer Confucius a job. However, since they were the two men currently holding their own Decisive Duke under a state of house arrest, Confucius was in a quandary. At one point, he even considered accepting their offer of a position on the understanding that he could do more good as part of a corrupt organisation than as someone who was not part of anything.

Set your heart upon the true path,
support yourself with righteous-
ness, wear goodness upon you, seek
distraction in the arts.

ANA: VII, 6

Gongshan Furao, who was then in open defiance of the ruling families of Lu, sent an invitation to Confucius. Implicit in the communication was the offer of political patronage – Gongshan had seized control of a town that belonged to the ruling families of Lu, and perhaps hoped to set himself up as the state's new ruler.

Confucius was in an unenviable position, waiting for a noble employer, only to find the original usurpers now themselves about to be usurped. If Gongshan were successful, Confucius might have a chance of a post in the new order, but if he did so, he would be betraying his own rules of propriety. Instead of abstaining from action, he would actively defy the rulers of Lu.

Our ancestors were careful in their speech, for fear that their actions would not support it. The cautious seldom err. The virtuous are slow in words and true in deeds.
ANA: II, 33–34

Confucius began to consider the offer seriously, but was stopped by the arguments of Zilu. As one of the eldest disciples, it is likely that only Zilu was brave enough, or foolhardy enough, to stand up to him. 'But,' Confucius said, 'surely he has invited me to see him for a reason?' Confucius was aching to put his theories into practice, and tried to reason with Zilu, pointing out that if he was right, his influence ought to make any state eventually transform itself into something wonderful, perhaps even as glorious as the capital of the dynasty itself. 'If anyone makes me the offer,' he said, 'with my help they could become like the Eastern Zhou.'

At least Confucius actually considered the offer from Gongshan Furao before rejecting it. Other offers were treated with even greater disdain. One of his former pupils, an academy drop-out named Ru Bei, came to see Confucius, pleased that he had somehow obtained a minor government post for himself. Confucius, however, refused even to see him, and sent one of his disciples to say that he was engaged on important matters, and unable to allow the caller to pay his respects. But as Ru Bei heard this inform-ation at the doorway, Confucius made a point of striking up a song on his lute and performing in a loud voice.[21] He made it very clear to the unwelcome caller that his current activity was anything but important, but certainly a more pressing matter than chatting with a pupil who had rejected his teachings.

The ultimate boss of all these callers was Yang Hu, the minister who still held sway over the Decisive Duke. Although Yang Hu tried to hire Confucius, Confucius would not forgive him for his efforts at undermining the Shining Duke during his long period of exile.[22] He was keen to bring Confucius into the government, and when Confucius made himself deliberately unavailable, Yang Hu was forced to resort to underhand means. He sent Con-fucius the gift of a pig, which arrived at Confucius's house when the philosopher was away. By Con-fucius's own strict rules of protocol, this now obliged him to pay a courtesy call on Yang Hu.

But Confucius knew the rules of propriety better than anyone else, and also knew ways around them.

He realised that he could avoid getting into a political discussion with Yang Hu if he in turn managed to arrive at a time when the corrupt minister was out. Timing his journey carefully, Confucius set out for Yang Hu's house, practising his look of feigned dismay when Yang Hu turned out to be absent. However, by luck or by judgement, Yang Hu was travelling on the same road. 'Come, let me speak with you,' he said, although the *Analects* records no reply from Confucius. 'Is it right,' Yang Hu pressed, 'that a good man should hoard a precious jewel, clutching it to his breast while his native land falls into confusion?'[23]

'No,' was Confucius's terse and reluctant response.

'And is it wise', Yang Hu continued, 'for a man to be anxious for public office, and yet constantly lose the opportunities of attaining it?'

'No', came the reply.

'The days and months are passing away', said Yang Hu. 'We are not getting any younger.'

'Fine,' Confucius is reported as saying. 'I will go into office.'

Although this is word for word how his return to government is reported in the *Analects*, Confucius still did not work for Yang Hu. But after fifteen long years of corruption, matters came to a head in 501 BC. One of Confucius's graduates would argue that it was inevitable – nobles were ignoble, ministers exceeded their authority, corruption was rife, and eventually the culprits would pay the price. By 501 the three noble families of Lu had tired of their ministers' constant jockeying for power, and took back control of the country. Money, in the end, was the deciding factor – the families had larger treasuries to draw upon, and Yang Hu and his fellow corrupt ministers found their support eroding.

Gossip and the spreading of rumours runs against the path of true virtue.

ANA: XVII, 14

Eventually, Yang Hu and Gongshan Furao were forced to flee for their lives across the border into Qi. The Decisive Duke regained control of his domain, and appointed a new, strong individual to replace the disgraced Yang Hu. The new chief minister was a pupil of Confucius, the boisterous, argumentative Zilu, and it would seem that Zilu did not forget his former teacher.[24] Before the end of the year, Confucius was offered a position in the government of the Decisive Duke, now restored to his true authority. After long years of teaching, the philosopher finally had the chance to put his theories into practice, as chief magistrate of his own town.

4

Statesman and Minister

At fifty, I accepted the fate decreed by
Heaven. *ANA*: II, 3

It was time for Confucius to put his theories to the
ultimate test. He was given control of the town of
Zhong-du and its immediate environs. Although the
name implies a central location (*zhong* means
'the middle'), the town appears to have been in the
outlying regions of Lu, somewhere near the border
with Qi.[1]

The political thinker had been given a remote
town, presumably somewhere close to the lawless
borderlands where once he had discussed tyranny
with a grieving widow. It was a tough assignment,
but it made political sense – at least he would be
unable to do much damage if he proved to be an
inept failure.

Confucius pushed his approved protocols on the
local population, insisting on the performance of
the correct songs at ceremonies, and the correct

behaviour of people towards one another. He demanded due reverence for the ancestors, both within the family and within the race as a whole, and in his selection of songs and rites he encouraged the dissemination of knowledge.

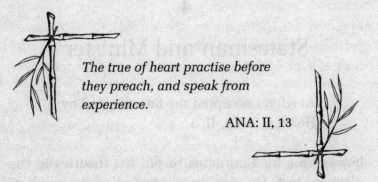

The true of heart practise before they preach, and speak from experience.

ANA: II, 13

Science and technology have appropriated much within the *Book of Rites* that had a basis in fact; we no longer need a song to tell us the best time to sow crops or bring in our nets. The popular cultures of later times and dynasties have overridden much of the *Book of Songs*. Modern times have new heroes to imitate, and new idols to set examples. The most obvious remnants of the ancient knowledge that Confucius prized so highly are now mere shadows of their former selves – Chinese astrology, fortune-telling from the *Book of Changes*, and the geomancy of *feng shui*. This latter discipline, for example, was once a subject of incredible importance, incorporating elements of geography, meteorology and archi-

tecture. Beneath the arcane explanations and
legends that informed it lay actual, practical knowledge used for siting buildings, predicting the
weather and planning towns. Now, its most visible
relics are simply superstitions.

When Confucius spoke of the 'kings' of old, he
referred to truly primitive peoples. Whereas the
English term summons up images steeped in medieval
feudalism, Confucius's kings of yore are considerably
further back in the timeline of human development:

Formerly the ancient kings had no houses. In
winter they lived in caves which they had
excavated, and in summer in nests which they
had framed. They knew not yet the transforming
power of fire, but ate the fruits of plants and trees,
and the flesh of birds and beasts, drinking their
blood and swallowing [also] the hair and feathers.
They knew not yet the use of flax and silk, but
clothed themselves with feathers and skins.[2]

Confucius stressed throughout his career that peril-
ously little separated mankind from such cave-
dwelling forebears. The only thing that kept humanity
from barbarism was a continued respect for knowledge, and, above all things, its preservation for later
generations. Confucius instilled in his pupils, and in
his new charges in Zhong-du, the debt they owed to
the wisdom of their forebears. At some point in the
past, someone had discovered fire, and because that
knowledge was not allowed to die, some later inventor

had used fire to fashion metal and pottery. Such developments led eventually to better tools, and they in turn led to the construction of houses, or the ability to cook food, allowing it to be preserved or seasoned. From textiles to armour, everything that Chinese civilisation prized issued in a line of innovation from the discovery of fire.[3] Confucius's teachings were an attempt to lock such knowledge in the heads of modern folk – language itself was the most prized of possessions, allowing current generations to build on the achievements of their forebears.

The rules in the *Book of Rites* took many forms, and at their most familiar simply repeat incidents of proverbial common sense. Boys were dissuaded from climbing trees or approaching the edges of cliffs. Parents must never tell lies in front of their children. Students should not interrupt their teachers while they were speaking. Good posture and deportment were encouraged. Travellers should make sure they knew how laws differ in foreign lands. Customers at inns were admonished not to expect everything on the menu to be available, nor to get angry about it.[4]

The *Book of Rites* was also explicit on the nature of gentlemanly conduct. It dictated the accepted manner of dressing for dinner and correct forms of address to one's superiors. A ruling monarch was expected to pay his respects to local centenarians. In Confucius's time, it was considered presumptuous to address a lady by her personal name, and rude to present a knife to another blade-first. When a messenger arrived, there was a dress code for receiving him – a means of reminding the recipient that the messenger spoke with the authority of the sender.

Other rules sound stranger, and remind us that we are dealing with very different times. The *Book of Rites* states that 'one should not live under the same Heaven with the enemy who has slain his father', encouraging vendettas, but also a nascent sense of justice – knowing that a victim's family would be obliged to seek revenge, perhaps a would-be murderer might think twice.[5] There are elaborate rules for the positioning of banners in chariots, to aid with identification of troop movements, and also the correct rules of the road for charioteers driving esteemed dignitaries.

Ruling by moral example will make you like the Pole Star, which remains firm in place while the other stars revolve around it.
ANA: II, 1

The *Book of Rites* truly deals with every conceivable aspect of life in sixth-century China. One of its chapters even contains detailed guidelines for dealing with fruit pips in polite company, or how to slice a melon.[6] All of the above rules and regulations were familiar to Confucius. Most of them were in existence long before his birth although many transgressors, such as the despised Jisun clan, only followed the maxims with which they concurred. It was Confucius who compiled and codified the *Book of Rites*, and, by all accounts, it was he who insisted on their enforcement in the town of Zhong-du.

> *Righteousness is not so far away.*
> *Wish for it to be so, and righteous-*
> *ness shall be by your side.*
> ANA: VII, 29

Much to the surprise of many, it seemed to work. Before long, Zhong-du was the flagship town for the region, and other population centres began to imitate Confucian policies. It was said that an article dropped in the streets of Zhong-du would not be stolen, but would instead be found by its owner exactly where he left it. Men and women kept polite distances from each other. Funeral customs were streamlined, and ostentatious burials became a thing of the past. The Confucian experiment was a success, and as such it did not go unnoticed by the Decisive Duke.[7]

Confucius was recalled to the Duke's court, where he was promoted to the title of Assistant Minister for Public Works, one of three branches of the Lu civil service – the others being Civil Affairs and Military Affairs. It was a relatively minor post, but it kept him at the centre of government, where he was able to speak directly with the Decisive Duke.

The *Analects* preserves one of their debates, in which the Duke asked Confucius whether there was a single slogan that could make a nation flourish. 'It takes more than one sentence to have such an effect', Confucius replied. 'However, it is often said that "being a ruler is hard, and ministers face many difficulties." If a ruler takes this phrase to heart, and does not expect his job to be easy, prosperity may ensue.' The Duke then asked if there were a slogan that could bring a country down. Confucius replied: 'It takes more than one sentence to have such an effect, unless the ruler says to himself – "The only good thing about being in charge is that nobody opposes me." If the ruler is wise and nobody opposes him, then it makes no difference. But if he makes mistakes and nobody opposes him, this attitude will eventually destroy his country.'[8]

Confucius, however, did not give up teaching during this period. He gained a new teenage protégé in the form of his disciple and assistant Yan Hui,[9] a cousin on his mother's side. Yan Hui was the diametrical opposite of the argumentative Zilu. Where the brash Zilu was a former soldier who thought of Confucius as a peer, the shy young Yan Hui only knew him as the revered teacher and minister. 'Yan Hui is no help to me', Confucius once joked, 'because he always agrees with everything I say.'[10] Nevertheless, Confucius doted on the boy, since he saw that the quiet, reserved youth internalised everything he learned. 'I can talk with Yan Hui all day, and he will nod at everything I say, as if he were an idiot', Confucius said. 'But when he goes home, I watch the way he behaves away from me, and I see that he puts my teachings to their proper use. That Hui is not foolish at all.'[11]

In the shy, retiring Yan Hui, Confucius saw a diplomatic wisdom very different from the bumptious face he himself had presented to the world as a younger man. He saw that silence often had its advantages. 'When my presence is required,' he said to Yan Hui, 'I come forth. When it is not, I do not show my face. You and I are unique in that regard.'[12]

However, the old Confucius still made his presence felt. When the body of the Shining Duke was returned to Lu for burial, it was interred in the cemetery of the Duke's ancestors. However, certain members of the Jisun clan, unable to lay aside the enmity that had consumed them all their lives, ordered that the Duke's tomb be placed at a distance from the others. It was an insult literally beyond the grave, using the rules of *feng shui* to shun the Shining Duke, so that even in death he might not find peace.[13]

Confucius was in a quandary. As minister for Public Works, the interment was one of his duties, but, as a former servant of the Shining Duke, he could not bear to cause his late lord any undue suffering in the afterlife. Eventually, he found a compromise solution, and did as he was ordered. But once the grave was dug and the Shining Duke laid to rest, Confucius ordered the digging of a ditch to surround the entire cemetery. By delineating a boundary that incorporated both the original ancestral tombs and the isolated Duke, the ditch made them one unified whole again.

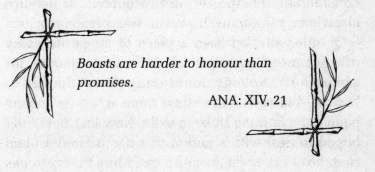

Boasts are harder to honour than promises.

ANA: XIV, 21

The leader of the Jisun clan demanded to know Confucius's intent, and Confucius told him straight that it was his way of atoning for his own disloyalty to his former master. It was a tense moment, but Confucius somehow got away with it. He had successfully manipulated protocol to save his face and his own skin, and such a stand seems to have impressed even those who disliked him.

In 500 BC, Confucius was called to attend the most important meeting of his career, guaranteed to test every element of his knowledge. The Decisive Duke was heading to the village of Jiagu for an important summit with the ruler of another state. After more than a century of antagonism, guarded détente and renewed belligerence, the state of Qi announced it was finally prepared to enter into a lasting treaty with Lu. This was good news for the Decisive Duke, as he would at last be able to secure guarantees from his opposite number the Honoured Duke. Qi accounted for over half of Lu's borders, so an agreement between the two nations would free up considerable manpower and resources for defence elsewhere. Confucius, however, was suspicious.

Qi, after all, had been a place of refuge for every disenchanted member of Lu's government for generations. Nobody could deny that – Confucius himself had spent some time there when he accompanied the Shining Duke in exile. Now Lu's new ruler hoped to deal with a nation that had offered asylum to some of his worst enemies, including the traitorous former ministers Yang Hu and Gongshan Furao.

It was understood that both dukes could bring their favoured ministers as assistants for the summit, to ensure that correct protocols were followed. Confucius was the obvious choice to accompany the Decisive Duke, and he was selected as the Master of Ceremonies. However, his presence in the Lu delegation was not welcomed by the men of Qi, many of whom remembered him from his earlier sojourn in their country. Confucius's suspicions were well-founded, since the men of Qi had every intention of hijacking the summit.

*Advise friends loyally and guide
them to the best of your ability.
If they pay no attention, then stop,
or you risk embarrassment.*
ANA: XII, 23

Even if they had not planned on doing so before, once they heard that the Duke's companion would be the reviled Confucius, they plotted to kidnap the Decisive Duke. They planned to arrange a distraction through third parties, namely the barbarian inhabitants of the region, which was of course excusably lawless. The Qi delegation persuaded a group of local barbarians to head for the meeting place and seize the Decisive Duke. Confucius, however, saw the approaching soldiers, and immediately raised the subject. 'Our two princes have come in peace', he said accusingly to the rival delegation. 'If you have brought savages to disturb this conference, it is no way for Qi to bring law and order to the kingdom. Such men have no place in a meeting between cultured representatives.

They are your underlings, and not empowered to participate. Moreover, weapons are forbidden at a summit – their presence is an affront to the gods, and contrary to common decency. In human terms, it is also rather rude.'[14]

Confucius's appeal to the laws of protocol forced a reply from the ruler of Qi. The Honoured Duke could no longer sit there at the summit and feign ignorance of the purpose of the approaching men. True enough, they were barbarians, but they were also his subjects, and they were advancing on the meeting place while bearing arms. The laws of protocol demanded that he order them away, and he did so.

In judging criminal cases, I am
impartial like any other. But surely
it is better to have no crimes at all.
ANA: XII, 13

Negotiations proceeded on the treaty, and Confucius was able to gain further ground with the rattled ambassadors of Qi. In return for amity, Qi demanded that the Decisive Duke agree to send 300 chariots in support of any campaigns Qi might take against a common enemy. On behalf of his lord, Confucius

Confucius in his prime, from a nineteenth-century Korean manuscript. Many of the best images of Confucius can be found outside mainland China, where his teachings have not been subject to the same fluctuations in favour. *(British Library, Or.11515 f.27)*

孔子十哲

顔淵　閔子騫　冉伯牛　仲弓　宰我　子貢　冉有　季路　子游　子夏

Eleven Disciples of Confucius. From left to right: Zixia, Ziyou, Zilu, Ran
Qiu, Zigong, Ziwo, Zhonggong, Ran Bo Niu, Min Sun and Yan Hui. From
Bunpô, *Bunpô Kanga*, 1803. *(Private Collection)*

孔子

子路

Confucius (right) and
Zilu. Masayoshi (Keisai),
Shôshoku Gakyo, 1794
(detail). *(Private
Collection)*

A qilin is the mythical creature said to
herald the birth or death of a sage.
Shunboku, *Gashi Kayô*, 1754.
(Private Collection)

Confucius at work. This illustration incorrectly has him writing on paper, a commodity not invented until 114 AD. Confucius 'wrote' his books by carving them into bamboo strips. Hokusai, *Ehon Chūkyō*, 1834. *(Private Collection)*

Zilu carrying a sack of rice to his parents, reading by moonlight as he tramps
barefoot along a lonely road. Yoshitoshi, *Tsuki Hyakushi*, 1888.
(© Asian Art and Archeology, Inc. / Corbis)

先聖孔子像

An engraving of Confucius. Note the long fingernails which denote a
scholar who does not have to work with his hands, and the hairy ear –
symbol of one who keeps his own counsel. Settei, *Wakan Meihitsu:
Kingyoku Gafu*, 1771. *(Private Collection)*

Korean dancers celebrating the birthday of Confucius.
(© Nathan Benn / Corbis)

The entrance to Confucius's tomb, Qufu. *(Robert Harding)*

The Tomb of Confucius. *(Robert Harding)*

The shrine at Confucius's tomb, Qufu. *(Robert Harding)*

agreed, but appended a rider. In return, Qi was forced to secede a contested territory north of the Wei river, which passed back into the hands of Lu.

It was an unprecedented diplomatic coup. The promised 300 chariots were only an abstract concept that did not require immediate delivery, whereas the real estate was palpable – Confucius had conquered part of Qi without a single casualty.

The Honoured Duke, hoping to seize the advantage when his rivals were otherwise occupied, suggested that the two new 'allies' should seal their agreement with a lavish celebration. Confucius gracefully declined, reminding the men of Qi that, according to the strict rules of protocol, such an entertainment would be unseemly after so solemn a contract. He then hurried his lord out of the dangerous situation before anyone could protest.

Finally Confucius had been able to demonstrate the power of learning in action, and he was soon rewarded with further promotion, to the post of Minister of Justice. It was possibly the highest rank available to a commoner in the state – since the Ministries of Public Works, Military Affairs and Civil Affairs were each commanded by a hereditary appointee from each of the three clans.

The thorniest case presented during his tenure was one in which a father sued his own son. It tested the very foundations of Confucius's teachings, since the Master had drilled his disciples for years on the primary importance of filial piety. Children were obliged to serve their parents with utmost devotion –

the strict rules of propriety for mourning were merely an outward manifestation of the type of respect for elders that Confucius's teachings demanded. For Confucius, the family home was a microcosm of the state itself, and if children were obeying their parents, and parents were obeying their government, and the government was in the hands of just and honourable men serving an enlightened ruler, then there could be no discord under Heaven.

However, the case of the father's suit brought Confucius's rhetoric to a staggering halt. He consulted with his advisers, argued it out with a few former pupils, and then left both father and son in jail for three months. At the end of their incarceration, he planned to simply release them both. Seeing this for the compromise it was, the Decisive Duke demanded an explanation. 'You once said that in a state or in a family, filial duty was the first thing to be insisted on. What hinders you now from putting to death this unfilial son as an example to all the people?'

Confucius's reply cut to the heart of his philosophy. 'There is no justice', he replied, 'if we execute underlings for the failings of their superiors. This father has not taught his son to be filial – listening to his charge would require the punishment of the blameless. The manners of this age have long been in a sad condition; we cannot expect the people not to be transgressing the laws.'[15]

For Confucius, 'duty' was a two-way street. Sons were obliged to be loyal to their fathers, and commoners to their lords, but the authority figures had duties of their own. It was the first occurrence of a doctrine that would later be known as *noblesse oblige* – the idea that privilege brought its own responsibilities. 'To keep order in the world,' wrote an ancient Confucian scholar, 'you must keep order within your family. You cannot teach others if you cannot even teach your own flesh and blood. Without even leaving your home, you can improve the world. Where filial piety is encouraged, the rulers shall be honoured. Where younger children acknowledge their duty to the elder, there shall be harmony in the world at large. Where there is kindness within the home, it shall spread through the mass of the people.'[16]

I have searched in vain for someone who is capable of seeing their own faults, and bringing the charge against themselves.

ANA: V, 26

In the generations that came after Confucius, many forgot this most central of his teachings. The Mandate of Heaven often came to be seen as a divine right to do whatever one pleased, and to establish absolute authority. In fact, however, implicit in the very foundations of Confucian thought is the idea that such a mandate can be revoked. Just as the tyrants of old were overthrown because they abused their power, Confucianism cautioned its adherents to do right by those less fortunate than themselves.

The true of heart help others achieve their good wishes. The wicked only help others enact their ill will.

ANA: XII, 16

The case also illustrates one of Confucianism's fundamental flaws. Like any theoretical system, it is prone to human error. It posits the way that things were supposed to work in a harmonious utopia, but was imposed upon a world of mere mortals. When pressed on this in later life, Confucius even provided a timescale: 'If someone were to employ me,' he said. 'we would see positive effects after twelve months. Within three years, we would have perfect government.'[17] But even Confucius recognised that perfect government would not result in overnight success.

'It is said that with good people in charge, one after the other, for a hundred years, there would be no need for capital punishment,' he conceded, 'for thieves and murderers would be a thing of the past. But even if a truly virtuous leader arises, it would still take time – perhaps a whole generation for virtue to prevail.'[18]

In other words, Confucius was fighting a losing battle. He had achieved much in office, but did not stay in his post for the minimum three years required. His use of the word 'employ' also carried with it a sense of obligation in both directions – he would carry out his responsibilities, but he expected his noble masters to approve his decisions. While the three clans enjoyed watching Confucian reforms reap positive benefits in their country, they were less keen to allow changes that affected them directly.

Confucius, however, pushed for full reform. He argued that one of the greatest problems in the state of Lu stemmed from the antagonistic relationship between the three clans. In much the same way as the dukes could ignore the decrees of the distant King when it suited them, the ruler of Lu often found his fellow nobles defying him. The 'Mandate of Heaven', such as it was in Lu, only allowed the nobles to command the commoners. The Decisive Duke himself was unable to command the lesser nobles with any efficacy, because at the first sign of an unwelcome decree, his relatives would threaten revolt. This, in turn, was made easier because of the martial footing in Lu – each of the clans possessed heavily fortified towns allowing them to mount an armed resistance.

Confucius wanted to change all that. He wanted to pull down the fortifications of the clan cities, so that only the Duke possessed a defensible site. Such a measure, while initially unwelcome, would strengthen the Duke's hold over his vassals and prevent them from opposing any further reforms. It would also prevent upstarts like the lately departed Yang Hu from seizing towns and using them to foment revolt.

If you are courteous, your friends will not dare to be rude. If you do the right thing, others will have to follow your example. If you are always true, others will not dare to be false.

ANA: IV, 13

The noble families, of course, hated the idea, but the Decisive Duke saw its merits. His advisers agreed it would be an excellent idea – unsurprisingly, since by this time both Zilu and Ran Qiu, the one-time idle student, had become government officials.

Thanks to the support of his clique and the Duke, Confucius was able to institute the first phase of his

scheme. The Shusun clan complied almost immediately, but Confucius ran into trouble with the Jisun
clan, whose city was in the hands of a former ally of
Yang Hu. The Jisun clan put up a fight, sending out
an army against the Decisive Duke's capital.[19]

It must have been a terrifying moment for Confucius, seeing the concrete, palpable result of his
protocols – an army advancing towards him. It was a
brutal reminder to the philosopher that until such
time as he had his century of perfect government,
political issues would still be decided and backed
by armed men.[20]

The Decisive Duke was forced to hide with his
ministers in a tower, while his soldiers fought with
the attacking Jisun clan. Eventually, the ruler's
forces were successful, and the walls of the town
were pulled down.

That only left the Mengsun clan, whose ruler
proved just as reluctant. Ironically demonstrating
exactly why Confucius disapproved of fortified
vassal towns, the leader of the Mengsun clan
changed his mind and sat in resolute defiance behind his well-defended walls. The Decisive Duke
sent soldiers to besiege the town, in a stand-off that
wore on and on, eventually undermining Confucius's
good standing at the court.[21]

The Mengsun clan would eventually retain its
walls, but by that time Confucius was not around to
protest. Two years into his role as the Minister of
Justice, he was forced to face another enemy he
could not defeat.[22]

Over the border in the state of Qi, its ruler the
Honoured Duke was still smarting from the embar-
rassing conference. He was also considerably worried
about the demilitarisation reforms Confucius was
busily instituting. However unpleasant the process, if
successful they would ultimately fuse Lu into one
single cohesive state, instead of the patchwork of rival
families it had always been. Without separate towns
to defend, the people of Lu would be forced to unite
in a single common goal – the defence of their entire
realm. The only wall worth holding would be the 'Qi
Wall' that ran along the border separating the two
states. Qi would no longer be able to play off family
against family and would be forced to withdraw from
areas of disputed territory.[23] This, as the court of Qi
agreed, was all the fault of that upstart Confucius.
More worryingly for them, if the three clans were
forced to present a united front, the military might of
Lu could effectively triple in size. Standing armies
trained to fight each other would suddenly be at a
loose end. While Confucius's well-intentioned followers were in charge, this would not be a problem,
but what if a more martial Duke took over the state?

The Honoured Duke was ready to shrink his
borders back to a more defensible position when he
was stopped by his adviser, Li Zi. As a last-ditch
measure, Li Zi suggested killing with kindness. If his
plot failed, then the Honoured Duke could consider
offers of territory.[24]

As a token of 'mutual admiration', the Honoured
Duke sent Lu sixty dappled ponies and eighty

dancing girls. It was the women who were the secret weapon, hand-picked for their astounding beauty and dressed in the finest clothes available. True to the rules of propriety, Lu's Decisive Duke made no attempt to receive them, but the leader of the Jisun clan sneaked out of town to see for himself. He reported the women's desirability to the Decisive Duke, who was unable to resist.[25] 'Master, it is time to leave,' said Zilu, his military upbringing apparently leaving him with an intuitive sense of danger.[26]

The true of heart are not unyielding, but only unyielding when they are right.

ANA: XV, 36

Confucius, however, was prepared to give his master the benefit of the doubt. 'The Duke will soon be sacrificing to Heaven and earth', he said. 'If he presents portions of the offerings to the ministers, I can stay.' Confucius's faith in his master's piety was unfounded. In fact, there weren't any sacrifices for three days. Instead of performing his sacred duties in the rituals that maintained harmony between

Heaven and earth, the Decisive Duke and his cronies busied themselves with their new playthings.

Confucius was deeply distrustful of the new arrivals, rightly believing them to be agents of Qi deliberately sent to drive him and the Decisive Duke apart. His last act in his brief political career was a public resignation, designed to shame the nobles into paying attention.

The nobles did not ignore Confucius's departure, but had other things on their minds. Half-heartedly, the leader of the Jisun clan sent a messenger after the departing Confucius, inquiring after his sudden departure. It was what Confucius had hoped for – he had made it easy for the messenger to catch up with him by staying overnight in a nearby town instead of hastening on the road. His reply, carefully calculated not to point fingers or name names, came in the form of one of the many old verses he had learned in his compilation of the *Book of Songs*:

> A woman's tongue
> Can cost a man his post
> A woman's words
> Can cost a man his head.[27]

Confucius was in no mood to hang around while courtesans from an old enemy enticed the Decisive Duke into decisions he might later regret. Though the leader of the Jisun clan expressed some small remorse at having caused Confucius's resignation, the dancing girls stayed, and Confucius left.

5

Exile

At sixty, I listened to what was right. *ANA*: II, 3

Confucius said: 'It is a pleasure to learn, and to put your learning to its appropriate use. It is a delight to receive friends from afar. It is a quality of the true of heart that they do not care they are not famous.' These are the words that begin the very first chapter of the *Analects*. They are one of his most famous quotes, and are often cited by Chinese hosts hoping to make visitors feel welcome, even today. They are also likely to have their origin in the period after Confucius's fall from grace, when he was forced to wander from kingdom to kingdom, peddling his advisory services – not a statement by a generous host, but a plea by an itinerant guest.

To the south was Song, the state where Confucius's family had fled a blood-feud. To the north was Qi, the state whose intrigues had caused his recent downfall. But westwards, in Wei, Zilu's brother-in-law was a minister with the local government.[1]

When Confucius went to visit the state of Wei, a disciple was his chariot driver.

'There are already so many people here', said Confucius.

'How would you improve this situation?' asked the disciple.

'I would enrich them', Confucius replied.

'And after they are rich?'

'Then I would educate them', said Confucius.[2]

As far as Confucius was concerned, the people of Wei needed a considerable amount of education, because their ruler, the Spirit Duke, was such a wastrel. Confucius had once openly said that Wei's ruler was only kept in power by the diligence of his ministers since he himself was dissolute and unfit to rule.[3]

Confucius was asked if the true of heart should act kindly towards their enemies. Confucius said: 'If I did that, how should I act towards my friends? Meet kindness with kindness, but meet resentment with the merit it deserves.'

ANA: XIV, 34

Nevertheless, Confucius's fame preceded him. At the border of Wei, a local warden commiserated with the jobless philosophers. Clearly a fan of Confucius's teachings, the warden introduced himself to the travellers, and told them to hang on to their dignity. 'The world under Heaven has long been devoid of principle', he said, 'but Heaven will use your Master like a bell uses its tongue.'[4] They were kind words for an exile, and as Confucius was to discover within Wei itself, the border warden was not his only supporter.

The travellers stayed with Zilu's brother-in-law for a brief period before their presence became known to the Spirit Duke. He asked his assistants what kind of salary Confucius had drawn in Lu, and upon being told that Confucius received 60,000 measures of grain, approved the same sum for him again, leading to a brief spell for him as an adviser.[5]

Wei, however, was not a good place for Confucius. His attitude soon made him new enemies, and after ten months he found his position souring at court. It is unlikely that Confucius, the stickler for propriety, would make many friends in a place like Wei, particularly considering his open criticism of the state in earlier times. He made a brief attempt to leave the country, but found himself in even greater danger at a border region that had suffered greatly during Yang Hu's tenure. Even though Confucius and Yang Hu had been bitter rivals, Confucius was mistaken for his old enemy and had to run from an angry mob.[6] He was arrested and held prisoner for ten days, until Yan Hui arrived to retrieve him.

Upon seeing his favourite disciple, Confucius was palpably relieved.

'I thought you were dead', he said.

'Master,' came the reply. 'How could I die while you are yet living?'[7]

On his return to Wei, things actually got worse. In 494 BC, the Spirit Duke took as his wife Nanzi, a woman who was conducting a public affair with her own brother. To Confucius's astonishment, the incestuous relative was permitted to reside at court with the newlyweds, and the bizarre relationship was infamous throughout the land, where even the local peasants knew bawdy songs about it.[8]

Pursuing a policy of staying out of trouble, Confucius did his best to abstain from any public association with the couple, who were transgressing fundamental rules of propriety. However, the Lady Nanzi forced his hand by sending him a message, pointing out that it was considered polite for illustrious guests of her husband to visit her also and pay their respects.

Tempers were clearly getting frayed in Confucius's circle of disciples. After years of good-natured argument and bickering, Zilu was scandalised to discover that Confucius was going to visit Lady Nanzi. As far as Confucius was concerned, he had no choice in the matter, and was obliged to obey the summons – by his rules, his duty to Nanzi as a duchess outweighed his duty to admonish her by refusing. 'If I have done wrong, let Heaven be my judge', he snapped.[9]

When away from home, treat all you meet as if they are dignitaries. Show respect to the common people, as if you were at a solemn ceremony. Treat others as you would like to be treated. Then, there will be no strife, either in the home or in the country at large.

ANA: XII, 2

A messenger arrived from another country, inviting Confucius to visit a local warlord. Confucius saw it as a chance to put some of his theories to the test, but he was restrained by one of his eldest disciples, the obstreperous Zilu, who quoted his own words back at him. 'Master,' he said, 'formerly I have heard you say that a gentleman does not associate with those who choose to do evil.'[10] Zilu argued that Confucius would be betraying his own teachings if he was prepared to lower himself to consort with a man who had betrayed the very same protocols that Confucius valued so highly. The inclusion of the incident in the *Analects* shows how desperate the situation must have become, with Confucius openly contemplating a compromise, and having to be talked out of it by his disciple. Zilu may have been the butt of many jokes in the *Analects*, but on this occasion, he was the one in the right, and Confucius knew it.

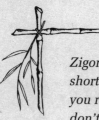

Zigong would often sneer at others' shortcomings. Confucius said: 'Are you really so perfect, yourself? I don't have time for this.

ANA: XIV, 31

Another incident reported in the *Analects* may also have its origins in this exile period, with neither Confucius nor his disciples holding out much hope of future promotion. Confucius said to his disciples: 'I am old, and soon will be of no further use. Many times I have heard you complain that nobody respects you. If some ruler *did* appreciate you and grant you employment, what would you do?'

Zilu was quick to reply, with a suitably martial response. 'I would like a nation with ten thousand chariots, under attack from several other countries, struck by a blight on its corn and a shortage of its other crops. It could be handed to me, and within three years, I would make its people bold and true of heart.'

Confucius smiled and asked the same question of Ran Qiu. He replied: 'I would want an area of sixty, no, seventy leagues on each side. Within three years, I could bring prosperity to the people. But I am no good at religious services or music, so someone else would have to do that.'

Confucius asked the same question of Gongxi Hua, who replied: 'I would like to help out at the temple services to the ancestors, and at the meetings of the king and his lords. Though I do not know how, I would be happy to learn.'

All three disciples had, in their own way, expressed a wish for political power, in one of the three ministries of Lu – Military, Civil and Public. Confucius turned to Zeng Xi, who was playing the zither at the time. 'I am not so ambitious', said Zeng Xi, standing up.

'That does not matter,' said Confucius. 'I still wish to hear your thoughts.'

'In that case,' said Zeng Xi, 'I'd quite like a day out. My friends and I, dressed in spring finery, could take some of the boys swimming in the river, enjoy the breeze up at the Rain Altar, and come home singing.'

Heaving a sigh, Confucius said: 'Zeng Xi has my vote.'[11]

While Confucius and his disciples sank further into penury, their absence from Lu did not go unnoticed. The Decisive Duke died in 494 BC, and was succeeded by his son, the Sorrowful Duke.[12] The leader of the Jisun clan sensed that his own end was near, and confessed to his heir that the country would be faring much better if Confucius had not left. It was a little late, but it was an admission that Confucius had been right to take such a drastic stand over the intrigues of Qi. As his health faded, the leader of the Jisun clan obliged his heir to make a revolutionary promise – to reinstate Confucius.[13]

However, such intentions did not long survive their creator. When the noble's son became the new prime minister of Lu, he began making plans to offer Confucius his old job, only to face opposition from other members of his government. The new prime minister was reminded that Confucius had already worked for Lu once before, and embarrassed the state with his resignation. If he were invited back again, only to resign once more, it would be a further cause for public ridicule.

Consequently, the government of Lu decided to hedge their bets by offering a post to a *Confucian*, but not to Confucius himself. Bitterly, Confucius sent Ran Qiu off to fill the post, and continued on his journey. 'Let *me* return', he is said to have said, to no avail.[14]

The disciple Zigong, however, made sure to take the departing Ran Qiu aside and tell him the obvious – that, if at all possible, he should attempt to have his Master reinstated in Lu.[15]

Confucius's travels took him to the large southern state of Chu, where a local potentate asked Zilu to describe his teacher. Zilu hesitated, but Confucius later said to him: 'You should have said I was just a normal man, who so loves the pursuit of knowledge, that its pursuit makes me forget to eat, and its attainment brings me joy, such that I forget my years.'[16]

An army can be deprived of its commander, but you cannot be deprived of your will.

ANA: IX, 26

He even approached the border of Song, the ancestral home of his family, where he was met with the most unwelcoming reception of his career. Confucius and his disciples were performing sacrificial rites beneath a large tree when they were disturbed by a group of men sent by a jealous minister. Supposedly, the minister had been discredited at the Song court by a Confucian scholar, and was determined to avenge himself on the architect of his demise. Local toughs were sent to pull the tree down with Confucius still under it, and the disciples were forced to scatter.

Zigong reached safety first, and spent an anguished few days in the state of Zheng, waiting to hear news of his master. Eventually, a messenger arrived to report a bedraggled visitor at the city gates, imposingly tall, but with the general appearance of a stray dog. When Confucius heard the description of himself, he laughed.[17]

You must be serious in daily life, attentive in your work, sincere in your dealings with others. Even though you may walk among barbarians, you should not let such concerns slide.

ANA: XIII, 19

The itinerant scholars eventually made their way even further south, to Chen, where they spent a year at the local court. There, Confucius impressed a local duke, who demanded to know who had killed a falcon on his land. The falcon in question had been shot with a strange arrow – eighteen inches long and tipped with flint. Confucius correctly identified the arrow as a Jurchen weapon, made by a tribe far to the north of the northernmost state of China. He went on to tell the story of the Martial King of the early Zhou dynasty, who had established contact with many outlying tribes, and demanded gifts from them. The Jurchens had sent such arrows as part of their tribute, and the arrows had eventually formed part of the dowry of the king's eldest daughter. Her husband, the current duke's ancestor, had also received the state of Chen itself as his wedding present. It was a moment of Holmesian deduction, as Confucius solved an apparent mystery, not by hunting and tracking down the falcon's killer, but instead locating him with the aid of nothing but a good grasp of history. Sure enough, the Duke found other Jurchen arrows in his own armoury. The falcon had been shot by one of his own nobles – perhaps even the Duke himself, seeking to test Confucius.[18]

Despite such feats, Confucius did not linger much longer in Chen. The state was attacked by three neighbours during his sojourn there, and he had no desire to outstay his welcome. Accordingly, he continued further to the south-west, until he arrived in Cai, a tiny ally of the much larger state of Chu.

The journey marked perhaps the lowest point of Confucius's travels, as he and his disciples idled the long hours with wish-lists of what they would like in an ideal world. Zilu said to Confucius: 'I wish I had chariots, horses and clothes of light fur, for if I did, I would share them with my friends, and not complain if they wasted them.'

'If my wish for success were granted,' said Yan Hui, 'I would not boast of my ability, or make a show of my achievements.'

'But what of you, great Master?' said Zilu. 'What do you wish for?'

Confucius replied: 'I wish for the elderly to find rest; for friends always to be true to one another, and for the young to be treated with kindness.'[19]

The light-hearted banter eventually ran out, along with their food and water. Hundreds of miles from their homeland, Confucius and his few remaining followers risked dying of starvation. As they limped ever onwards, hoping to find a place to obtain new supplies, Zilu took it particularly hard. 'Is this what the true of heart are supposed to endure?' he said, angrily.

'The true of heart may indeed have to endure such hardships as this,' said Confucius. 'But only the foolish would lose their self-control when it happens.'[20]

Eventually, after a few more stops, Confucius and his entourage drifted back to Wei. There, the Spirit Duke asked Confucius a question on martial matters, leading the sage to reply archly that he knew something about ritual, but not strategy.[21]

Life in Wei grew increasingly messy. The Spirit Duke's heir, a child of his first wife, had grown increasingly agitated because of the behaviour of his stepmother the Lady Nanzi. Eventually, he attempted to have her killed, and, when this failed, he was forced into exile. Soon after, the Spirit Duke died, causing a crisis of succession. With the true heir absent for attempted murder, the rulership passed instead to the Spirit Duke's grandson, the Excessive Duke.[22] However, the Excessive Duke was immediately opposed by his own father, who returned to the country to claim his birthright.

> *Our lives depend on righteousness.*
> *If we lose it but remain alive, we*
> *avoid death only by luck.*
>
> ANA: VI, 17

Confucius arrived in the middle of this dispute, and was immediately fêted by the pretender, who hoped to appeal to his sense of propriety. Confucius, however, refused to get involved in such a tangle – there was no way he was going to support either of the disloyal parties in public. Consequently, although Zilu had found employment in the Wei government and urged him to do likewise, Confucius went into seclusion once more, leaving a gap of several years in his biography. Presumably, for that time, he returned to his editing and compiling, and took no part in civil affairs.

Occasional emissaries from foreign lands would approach him asking for advice, but Confucius was unable to parley such embassies into real employment. The disciple Zigong suggested that Confucius should make more of an effort. Perhaps inadvisably, he used a similar analogy to the one that Yang Hu had once employed, asking Confucius if, owning a beautiful piece of jade, he would keep it hidden in a box, or sell it to a connoisseur. 'I would sell it! I would sell it!' said Confucius. 'But first I would need to find a worthy purchaser.'[23]

He even once mused that he should leave the civilised world completely behind, and find a totally barbaric 'state' to manage elsewhere, if it would have him. He suggested, perhaps only half in jest, that he should live out among the nine barbarian tribes, but his disciples feared he would find it hard to bear the customs and practices of uncultured people. Confucius said: 'For how long would they remained uncultured, if a gentleman were to dwell among them?'[24]

Zigong tried again on another occasion, suggesting that Confucius should make more effort to appease potential employers. 'What if someone is loved by everyone else in their village?' he asked.

'That proves nothing,' replied Confucius.

'What if someone is hated by everyone else in their village?'

'That proves nothing, either', said Confucius. 'Surely it would be better if someone is loved by all the good people, and hated by all the bad ones.'[25]

Confucius had come to realise that politics was not a popularity contest in a feudal state. No matter how wise or noble his rules and philosophy, he needed the backing of a truly powerful supporter to institute his schemes. Otherwise, his fame proved to be double-edged. Many would welcome him, but few would employ him. Ancient sources imply that Confucius visited almost all of the states that made up ancient China, but never found his ideal post. Even if a noble respected him enough to offer him a job, other retainers would fear for their own positions, afraid Confucius's strict protocols would find them wanting.

By 484 BC, his position in Wei was becoming untenable once more. A nobleman came to see Confucius, and demanded to consult him on his plans for a military campaign. Confucius refused, but the conversation seems to have become quite heated. Harsh words, it would appear, were said about Confucius's emigré status in Wei.

Eventually, Confucius climbed into his chariot and prepared to leave for good, angrily informing his inquisitor: 'The bird chooses its tree! The tree does not choose the bird!'[26]

Confucius, however, had little idea of where he could go next, having exhausted the hospitality of every other state in the region. He had burned all his bridges, either through telling people unwelcome truths, or simply because others feared him. The state of Chu employed Confucian scholars in all three of its ministries, but refused to offer him a post, for fear that his personal connection to the other officers would tempt him to lead a coup and make *himself* Duke.

It was, therefore, convenient that a messenger chose that moment to arrive from Confucius's home state of Lu. He bore a letter from the disciple Ran Qiu, who had been serving there for some years as a minister. Ran Qiu announced that all was well in Lu, and that the ruling clans were impressed with his institution of Confucian reforms. All was forgiven; if Confucius wished, he could return home.[27]

6

Sage

At seventy, I could do as I chose, knowing
I would not do wrong. *ANA*: II, 3

Confucius was now nearing seventy, and had spent
many years in exile. His retirement found him
treated with guarded respect by a generation of new
nobles that employed his former students. But
Confucius's latter days were bittersweet, tinged with
tragedy, a sense of wasted years and a genuine fear
that all he had accomplished would die with him. If
we are to believe contemporary sources, Confucius
believed that, of all his pupils, only Yan Hui had internalised his teachings in their entirety. The others
were still picking and choosing – the *Book of
History*, *Book of Songs*, *Book of Rites* and *Book of
Music* were slowly extending their influence, but
Confucius knew that many other elements of his
philosophy might not survive him. Consequently, he

began a final major project: the compilation of an extensive history of the state of Lu, designed to point out the many mistakes of his predecessors, in the hope that later generations would not repeat them.

The *Spring and Autumn Annals* dispassionately records the intrigues of Lu but was still regarded by many later generations as a reasonable indicator of the opinions of its alleged author – whoever wrote the book demonstrated a great desire to impugn unsuitable government and praise overlooked ministers.

Only in winter do the pine and cypress show they are evergreen.
ANA: IX, 27

Confucius had reason to feel overlooked. The *Analects* records several incidents when he was harangued by hecklers, including one late in his life when a local yokel taunted him about his celebrity. 'Confucius is great indeed,' said the man, 'but though he knows much about many things, he does not attempt to become famous for anything in particular.'

'Perhaps I should take up chariot-driving?' said Confucius sarcastically, since this might impress his critic more. 'Archery, maybe? No, chariot-driving.'[1]

Confucius was also understandably bitter about Ran Qiu. Although pleased that many of his disciples had found employment in other states, he did not always agree with their decisions. Ran Qiu annoyed him the most, since he essentially had the post that Confucius had once held himself. The former disciple added insult to injury by actively seeking Confucius's advice on a matter of taxation, and then ignoring it. Confucius was incensed, and wished for someone to arrest Ran Qiu like a common criminal. 'He is no disciple of mine!' said Confucius. 'Children, beat the drum and assail him!'[2]

One of the Jisun clan once asked Confucius to discuss great ministers, a subject which Confucius enjoyed. Consequently, the Master was somewhat put out when the clansman used Zilu, still serving in Wei, and Ran Qiu as his examples. 'I'm sorry,' Confucius said. 'I thought you wanted to talk about *great* ministers, but instead you want to talk about those two? To become a truly great minister, one must serve his ruler according to what is right, and if unable to do so, he must retire.' The pointed reference to his own earlier resignation was obvious. 'Those two, however, they are merely *reasonable* ministers.'

'They will always obey their chief?' the clansman asked.

'Not if he was planning a revolution,' said Confucius, who suspected that the clansman was.[3] Confucius had some difficulty in adjusting to the fact that his disciples now held the posts that he had once wanted for himself. He was particularly annoyed when he tried to query one of Zilu's decisions, and was told to back off. Back in Wei, Zilu had recommended the disciple Zigao for a position as a country magistrate. 'You are spoiling that boy', protested Confucius. 'You are forcing him to take office before he has acquired any learning.' Zilu, however, saw no need to waste any time teaching the appointee about court protocol, when he was eminently qualified to do the limited task at hand. 'The region already has common people and civil servants', he said. 'It has altars to the spirits of land and grain. Reading more books won't make him a better administrator.'

'This is why', Confucius replied, 'I cannot stand your facetious cronies.'[4]

The servant had become the master, and Confucius was forced to watch as Zilu made further decisions of which he disapproved.

Thanks to asides in the *Spring and Autumn Annals*, we know that although Confucius was welcomed in Lu, and occasionally had the ear of the respectful Sorrowful Duke, he had no official post. Instead, he busied himself with his writing and teaching, and developed a new interest in a work he had previously ignored – the *Book of Changes*, or *Yijing*. More commonly known today as the *I Ching*, the *Book of Changes* was already many centuries old in Confucius's time. It contained commentaries on sixty-four magical hexagrams, each providing an oracular answer steeped in mysticism. Court diviners would ask a question, and then select one of the sixty-four answers at random, interpreting its vagaries to reach an acceptable conclusion.

The wise do not promote people simply for what they say, nor do they ignore good advice simply because of who says it.

ANA: XV, 22

Supposedly, Confucius spent so much time poring over the manuscript that he wore out the leather thongs that held the bamboo strips together on three occasions.[5] Such interest was a great surprise to his disciples, who had heard him hector them many times about the follies of superstition. Zigong said to him: 'Master, long ago, you told us that an interest in spiritualism displayed a loss of virtue, and that a desire to know the future led to divination. I took your words to heart, and endeavoured to follow them. But now you are older, and you take delight in these things. Why?'

'The words of a gentleman are as precise in meaning as carpentry', said Confucius. 'I do not wish to see the future, merely the words of wisdom in the commentary itself. I read the *Book of Changes* for its essential truth, and for its wisdom of olden times. I do not use it to tell the future.'[6]

Those who do not think ahead, will soon find their troubles close at hand.

ANA: XV, 11

Confucius's academic interest in the *Book of Changes* may have been genuine, because he retained his former attitude towards other superstitions. The *Analects* reports an encounter between the ageing Confucius and an old friend of his, who had found solace in the contemplation of Daoism. Instead of paying his respects to a sage in meditation, Confucius accused him of 'squatting on his heels like a barbarian'. 'When you were young,' he said, 'you were arrogant and uncouth. When you became a man, you accomplished nothing of merit. Now you are old, you refuse to die. You are a pest.' And with that, Confucius hit him on the leg with his stick.[7]

In 481 BC, Confucius was called to consult on a matter of ducal concern. The Master irritably gathered up his finery and travelled to the western reaches of Lu, doubtless expecting his time to be wasted on another pointless question of superstition or strategy (subjects he refused to discuss), or protocol (on which he was tired of being ignored). Instead, it was a case of taxonomy; a minor noble had captured a strange creature during a hunt, and the wisest man in Lu had been called to identify it.

There is no pictorial representation of the beast in question, nor is there much clue in the ancient accounts as to what it actually may have been. But several accounts are unanimous in what Confucius thought it was, and the effect it had on him. On seeing the captured creature, Confucius began to weep. It was a *qilin*, the legendary beast said to herald the birth of a sage, or the death of one. Tied to its horn, so the story goes, was a frayed piece of ribbon. 'For whom have you come? For whom have you come?' sobbed Confucius. 'My time is over.'[8]

The sighting of the *qilin* was a great shock to Confucius. If it truly was an omen intended for him, it confirmed that he was indeed the throneless king his mother had dreamed of. But if that were the case, then he was also soon to die.

Before long he was taken ill with a disease serious enough to lead to a courtesy call from the Sorrowful Duke. On hearing that his overlord was coming to visit, Confucius insisted on dressing in his court regalia as a mark of respect. He eventually received the Duke in his full finery, lying on his bed with his head facing east, as protocol dictated.[9]

Confucius recovered from his ailment, but became increasingly haunted by signs of death and decay. The *Book of Rites* recounts an incident in which Confucius asks Zigong to dispose of his dead dog – an incident in which he muses absent-mindedly about propriety, while trying to hide his sense of loss. 'I have heard', he said, 'that a worn-out curtain should not be thrown away, but may be used to bury a horse in; and that a worn-out umbrella should not be thrown away, but may be used to bury a dog in. I am poor and have no umbrella. In putting the dog into the grave, you can use my mat; and do not let its head get buried in the earth.'[10]

Meanwhile, Confucius became a grandfather, with the birth of a son to Top Fish and his wife. The boy eventually became known as the philosopher Zisi, following in his grandfather's footsteps.[11] He would not, however, know his father, because Top Fish died that year at a relatively young age. True to the rules he had drawn up himself, Confucius refused to give his son an ostentatious funeral, insisting instead on a humble coffin and simple rites.

News came of unrest in Wei, where two of Confucius's disciples were still working as ministers. Confucius ruefully predicted that Zigao would escape with his life, but that the argumentative Zilu would meet with his death.[12] Sure enough, later reports indicated that Zilu was dead. The scandal-ridden rulers of Wei had entered another round of intrigues, resulting in the current ruler's widowed sister urging her servant-lover to organise a palace coup on behalf of a banished heir. True to his Confucian training, Zilu did not desert the incumbent Duke, but instead began making arrangements to escort him out of harm, into exile in Lu if necessary. His fellow Confucian Zigao advised him to flee, but Zilu continued to act in his lord's interest, and was mortally wounded during a fight in the palace. Contemporary sources report his last words, a lament that he was not attired in the proper manner.[13]

> *I hope that old people live lives free of cares, that my friends have faith in me, and that the young shall remember me when I am gone.*
> ANA: V, 25, iv

Confucius wept for the passing of his sparring partner of many decades, but nothing could have prepared him for an even greater bereavement that was to follow. Yan Hui, his favourite disciple, fell sick and died. He was barely in his thirties, and Confucius took his death harder than that of anyone else, including his own son. 'Alas! Heaven is destroying me! Heaven is destroying me!' Confucius said, mourning Yan Hui to such a great extent that other disciples asked him if he was not overreacting. 'Overreacting!' he said. 'If I do not mourn bitterly for this man, for whom should I mourn?'

The disciples decided to give Yan Hui a great funeral, but Confucius forbade them from doing so. Nevertheless, the disciples disobeyed him and buried Yan Hui in style, much to Confucius's anger. 'Yan Hui treated me as his father, yet I have not been able to treat him as if he were my son', said Confucius, referring to the modest funeral arrangements made for Top Fish. 'It is you, my disciples, who have failed us both.'[14]

There is more to life than cramming yourself with food all day. Play chess or something. Anything is better than nothing.
ANA: XVII, 22

Confucius was now convinced that his life's work would die with him, and that his many attempts to educate future generations would be diluted within a few generations. 'No one compared[15] to Yan Hui',

Confucius said. 'A handful of rice to eat, nothing but water to drink, and living in a squalid area would have been unbearable for most, but such conditions never had any effect on his cheerful nature. No one compared.'

In late spring 479 BC, Confucius fell ill again. The disciple Zigong, who seems to have become his attendant in his twilight years, found him hobbling on his staff near his door, quoting an ominous song:

> Mount Tai crumbles
> The great beam breaks
> The wise man withers away.[16]

Confucius had dreamt that he was sitting between two pillars with offerings before him – a vision that could only have made sense to a master of protocol. Although the imagery meant nothing in modern times, during the ancient Shang dynasty, from whom Confucius claimed distaff descent, it was the prescribed means of laying out a corpse at a funeral service.

Confucius already felt ill again, and he took to his bed once more. His last recorded words were bitter and doleful:

> No intelligent monarch arises; there is not one in the world that will make me his master. My time has come to die.[17]

Within a week, Confucius was dead.

He was buried north of Lu's capital, and the Sorrowful Duke insisted on delivering a eulogy. 'For now, Heaven will not relinquish our retired former minister', he said. 'Let him watch over me now, as I am a man alone in a position of command. With his departure, I am sick with loneliness. Father Confucius has left us. I have no example to follow.'[18]

Although heartfelt, the Duke's speech angered the surviving scholars of Confucius's academy. They were unimpressed with the Duke's show of emotion, since he had not valued 'Father Confucius' highly enough to give him anything except an honorary post during his lifetime. They were also insulted by the Duke's claim that he was now 'alone', since one of the central points of Confucius's life was to ensure that knowledge was transmitted to others. The Duke's words may have been good-natured hyperbole, but they were not well received.

The remaining disciples went into mourning for their Master, and then went their separate ways, all except Zigong, who stayed close to Confucius's grave for three further years. Later generations saw the compilation of the sayings of Confucius by his disciples and their descendants, leading to a growing tradition of scholarship and diplomacy. However, a perfect prince, ready and able to enforce the maxims of a perfect sage, never arose. As in the lifetime of Confucius himself, politically minded courtiers resisted any attempt to bring about enlightened rule through some nebulous idea of simply being good to each other. In the decades after Confucius's death, China was thrown into a series of bloody conflicts between its component states until 221 BC, when the westernmost nation of Qin finally conquered all the others.

The wise pick the right moment.
Then they exert all their strength
until the task is done, not resting at
the noon of day, nor in the twilight
of their years.

SDA, 15

The ruler of Qin, the first true emperor of China, was Confucianism's greatest enemy. He and his advisers were Legalists, devoted to the idea that men were inherently selfish, and required the firm hand of an authoritarian ruler. In 213 BC, a Confucian scholar protested that the emperor risked offending Heaven by riding roughshod over centuries of tradition. His comments angered the Qin emperor, who subsequently ordered a purge on scholars and scholarship.

It was one of the lowest points in the cultural history of China – an act of brutal philistinism that saw the burning of piles of books and scrolls, the suppression of any text that did not relate to medicine, agriculture or divination, and the execution of hundreds of learned men.[19]

But although the Qin emperor was able to conquer China, he was not able to hold on to it. His totalitarian regime collapsed within a generation, plunging China into chaos once more. By the time a new dynasty, the Han, gained control, the atrocities of the Qin regime were seen not as Confucianism's defeat, but as its vindication. Surviving scholars preached that Legalism had been tried and found wanting, and that now China's best hope lay in the institution of Confucian reforms and Confucian education.

Confucius did not say anything on the following subjects: extraordinary phenomena, amazing feats of strength, disorder and the spirit world.

ANA: VII, 20

Some history books record that Confucianism became China's 'state religion' at this point, although it was never a religion. Nor was it a recognisable school of thought – the ensuing centuries have seen endless argument about which surviving works are true 'Confucian Classics', and which are later forgeries. Over time, the sayings collected in the *Analects* and other sources have been reduced to a concept of eight Confucian virtues, for which the just are expected to strive: Benevolence, Righteousness, Courtesy, Wisdom, Fidelity, Loyalty, Filial Piety and Service to Elders.

Confucius called for a utopian perfection, a return to a mystical age which, if we are to believe existed at all, must also have ended in failure – a decline in virtue that led to the imperfect situation as Confucius found it in his own time. Despite this essential contradiction, later Chinese dynasties accepted that the Confucian way was a noble and worthy cause to which they should aspire.

Around the time of the birth of Christ, the Han dynasty's Emperor of Peace conferred a ducal rank on Confucius in the afterlife, and proclaimed him 'All-Complete and Illustrious'. By the end of the first century AD, scholars were sacrificing to Confucius as if he were a deity. Few works of Chinese philosophy do not take Confucius as their starting point, even if their conclusions oppose everything he said. Confucian scholarship also flourished in other Asian countries, particularly Korea and Japan, where the ideal of the gentleman-scholar became ingrained in the local culture – respect for the old/superior and duty to the young/inferior is a central part of oriental societies.

His philosophy spread and eventually reached Europe some 2,000 years after his death, where it gained the approval of influential Enlightenment thinkers. In China itself, an encyclopedic grasp of the Confucian classics was mandatory for any public official – the imperial examinations that tested this knowledge were only abolished in the twentieth century, shortly before the abdication of China's last emperor. Although Confucius fell out of favour in Communist China, he maintains his stature in Chinese communities elsewhere, and is revered as China's greatest philosopher. His thoughts on always doing the right thing, on returning the respect of others, and of striving to improve the lives of everyone with whom we come into contact, have become fundamental tenets of humanism.

The line Confucius draws, between *religion*, which is vital to the true of heart, and *superstition*, a pointless distraction, has been the cause of much debate, particularly over whether Confucianism is a religion. For Confucius, respect for one's fellow human beings, reverence for ancestors, and an understanding of higher powers were implicit. Empty ritual disgusted him; what mattered was that the worshippers meant what they said, and put it into practice in the world at large.

Two-and-a-half thousand years after he lived, the words of Confucius are just as relevant today. We live in an increasingly godless world, but one in which communication between the religious and the secular is becoming more common. Confucius offers a common ground for modern times, a sacred tradition that values true goodness, and calls for respect and honour in our daily dealings. Whichever god you believe has set the mystic Mandate, Confucius calls us all to turn our eyes away from the distant divine, and look around us at what we can do to make the world a better place.

Notes

ABBREVIATIONS

ANA: *Analects*
GL: *Great Learning*
DM: *Doctrine of the Mean*
SDA: *Several Disciples Asked*
KFMA: *Kong Family Masters' Anthology.*

INTRODUCTION

1. There is a touching naiveté in this assumption, ignoring as it does the concept that usurpers would seek to legitimise their grab for power after the event. The enemies of Confucius, the Legalists, would argue that the political arena simply favours the survival of the fittest.

2. For the best textual analysis of conflicting materials, see Brooks and Brooks (eds), *The Original Analects: Sayings of Confucius and His Successors*, a groundbreaking work that questions many former

119

assumptions – in fact, it questions so many of them
that one is tempted to trust nothing at all!

3. My translations from the *Great Learning* (Da Xue) and
   Doctrine of the Mean (Zhong Yung) use the Chinese
   text in Legge, *Confucius*, which is also the source for
   my translations of the *Analects* (Lun Yu).
4. Quotes from both the *Essentials* (Yao) and *Several
   Disciples Asked* (Er San Zi Wen) are taken from the
   Chinese text in Shaughnessy, *I Ching: The Classic of
   Changes*.
5. Brooks and Brooks (eds), *Original Analects*, p.3n,
   prefers 'prince'.

CHAPTER 1

1. Barnes, *Rise of Civilization in East Asia*, p.40, notes
   that all major oriental languages, including Chinese,
   refer to the past as something ineffably 'higher' than
   our present day.
2. Shang was the name used by the people of that nation,
   though their conquerors referred to them as the Yin,
   and that is the name by which they can be found in
   most Chinese sources. Chinese sources also cling to the
   term 'emperor' for the rulers of the period, although I
   have called them kings here. China's first true emperor
   was the infamous Qin Shi Huangdi, he of the terracotta
   army, who was not born until 258 BC.
3. Confucius grew up listening to stories of his ancestor's
   wisdom in avoiding conflict. He praises his pacifist
   action in *ANA* XVIII, 1.
4. Brooks and Brooks (eds), *Original Analects*, p.268,
   presents a convincing argument that Shuliang was

younger, and offers many alternative dates and readings, but I have stuck to conventional belief in this account.

5. Chang, *Life of Confucius*, p.59, is more specific, saying that Mang-pi was 'lame in one leg'. Confucius cared for his brother throughout his life, considering it part of his fraternal duty. During the same period, the people of Sparta were leaving disabled children to die on hillsides. *ANA* XV, 41, records an incident in which Confucius treats a blind musician with courtesy and compassion, whereas his disciples regard the man as nothing more than a bumbling servant.

6. Legge, *Confucius*, p.58.

7. Legge, *Confucius*, p.59n. The term *ye-he* as found in the *Records of the Historian* has been variously interpreted as 'torrid', 'common-law' or even simply as referring to a mating that took place 'in the wilderness'. It is far more likely to refer to their disparity in ages – Zheng-zai was barely fifteen at the time of the wedding, which was young even by the standards of the day. See also Chang, *Life of Confucius*, p.60. Confucius himself regarded the proper age for a girl's marriage as twenty. See Ariel, *K'ung-Ts'ung-Tzu*, p.76.

8. The term *Zhong* optimistically implies 'Second (of Three)', although Confucius proved to be his father's youngest child.

9. Zheng-zai appears to have kept the location of her late husband's grave secret from Confucius, such that at the time of her own death he was unable to bury them side by side for some time. See Yang and Yang (eds), *Records of the Historian*, p.1.

10. *ANA* XVII, 9.

11. *ANA* XIII, 5.
12. Chinese sources make the highly unlikely claim of 9ft 6in. Even allowing for the difference in size between an ancient Chinese 'foot' and its modern equivalent, this would still make him 7ft tall! Two metres is thus a conservative estimate, but not unknown in the area. The region of Confucius's birth is now the home of one of China's premier basketball teams.
13. *ANA* XVII, 25.
14. Duke Zhou (r. 541–510 BC), cited throughout this book by his posthumous title of *Zhao*, 'Shining'.
15. Carp is *Li* in Chinese. *Bo-yu* places the character for 'eldest of brothers' ahead of that for 'fish'. See Legge, *Confucius*, p.60.
16. Confucius may have had more children, but these are the only ones recorded. Of the daughters, we know of one because she married a disciple, and of the other because of the inscription on her grave.
17. The clans were descended from the first, second and third sons of a concubine of Duke Huan (r.711–694 BC), and were known in Chinese as the *Shu*, *Zhong* (*Chung*), and *Ji* (*Chi*) families – archaic terms for their ancestors' order of birth. The *Zhong* family later changed its name to *Meng* (Mang) for complex reasons of protocol. At the time of Confucius, it was the Jisun clan who had the greatest influence over affairs of state. See Legge, *Confucius*, p.147n.
18. For example, see *ANA* III, 1, 6; *ANA* VI, 7.
19. Mencius, quoted in Legge, *Confucius*, p.60.
20. Ibid.
21. See *ANA* IX, 30.
22. Legge, *Confucius*, p.115. Zilu (Tsze-lû) was also known as Zhong-yu or Ji-lu.

23. Sims, *Confucius*, p.12, claims that Confucius was orphaned at a much earlier age, and that the woman whose death he mourned at this point was an aunt.
24. *ANA* III, 26.
25. *Liji*, II, Section 1.i.10; Section 2.iii.30. Müller (ed.)/Legge (trans), *Sacred Books of China*, Vol. III, p.369. See also Legge, *Confucius*, p.62.
26. Legge, *Confucius*, p.62. The report of the visit, by the ruler of the small state of Tan, can be found in the *Spring and Autumn Annals*.
27. *ANA* III, 23.

CHAPTER 2

1. Legge, Confucius, p.63, places this event in 518. Yang and Yang (eds), *Records of the Historian*, p.2, claim it was when Confucius was a teenager, but they are forced to rely on the scatty ordering of their original Chinese source.
2. Ibid., p.64, discusses who may have accompanied Confucius on his mission.
3. Ibid., p.66, quoting the *Jiayu* or *Narratives of the School*.
4. Ibid.
5. Ibid.
6. Ibid.
7. *ANA* XI, 12.
8. *SDA*, 6.
9. Barnes, *Rise of Civilization in East Asia*, p.146, notes that horseback riding was not very common at this time.
10. Legge, *Confucius*, p.67.

11. There was a wall that marked a border between the countries, but on various occasions the border was either too far behind Qi territory, or too deep inside it.
12. *ANA* VII, 13.
13. Jing (Ching).
14. Yang and Yang (eds), *Records of the Historian*, p.3.
15. Legge, *Confucius*, p.68, reports several incidents in the *Jiayu*, but doubts their reliability.
16. Ibid., also quoting from the *Jiayu*.
17. *KFMA* II, 14. See also Ariel, *K'ung-Ts'ung-Tzu*, p.85.
18. *ANA* XII, 11.
19. Legge, *Confucius*, p.69. Legge would rather believe that Yan Ying did not say such words, but grudgingly concedes that to many of Confucius's contemporaries they did indeed sound like fair comment.
20. Yang and Yang (eds), *Records of the Historian*, p.4.
21. *ANA* XVI, 12.
22. *ANA* XVI, 6.
23. Ariel, *K'ung-Ts'ung-Tzu*, p.77.

CHAPTER 3

1. *ANA* III, 1.
2. *ANA* III, 2.
3. *ANA* III, 3.
4. *ANA* V, 17.
5. *ANA* V, 19.
6. *ANA* XVII, 26.
7. *ANA* II, 21.
8. *ANA* VIII, 13.
9. *ANA* VII, 8.
10. *ANA* VII, 7.

11. *ANA* V, 1. The pupil's given name was Gong Ye-chang.
12. *ANA* VI, 10. The pupil's 'scholar name' was Ziyou.
     I have called him Ran Qiu throughout to avoid
     confusion with another Ziyou among the disciples.
13. *ANA* V, 6.
14. *ANA* XVI, 13. Top Fish's other appearances in
     Confucian sources are limited to an anecdote in which
     Confucius admonishes him for mourning his mother
     for too long, and the later deliberations over the
     arrangements for his funeral.
15. Or so many of his supporters claim. In fact, however,
     Confucius seemed to spend most of his life oscillating
     between careers. On several occasions, he made it very
     clear that he would rather be in government.
16. *ANA* II, 2.
17. *ANA* IX, 30.
18. Yang and Yang (eds), *Records of the Historian*, p.6.
     Sources are divided as to when Confucius did what,
     but it makes sense that he worked on the central canon
     during this period, and then compiled the *Spring and
     Autumn Annals* and his annotated *Book of Changes* in
     his second 'retirement' period a decade later. See Yao,
     An Introduction to Confucianism, p.53.
19. Legge, *Confucius*, p.161. The Duke's given name was
     Song (Sung), but I refer to him throughout this book as
     Ding (Ting) the Decisive, which was his posthumous
     title. Chang, *Life of Confucius*, p.30, calls him Sung the
     Serene.
20. Sometimes also called Yang Ho.
21. *ANA* XVII, 20.
22. See Legge, *Confucius*, p.317n.
23. *ANA* XVII, 1. Even in classical Chinese, the passive-
     aggressive nature of Confucius comes across very

strongly here, with simple two-character responses to
Yang Hu's florid sentences.

24. Chang, *Life of Confucius*, p.29. On the other hand,
Legge, *Confucius*, p.74, claims that Zilu did not
get a government post until a couple of years
later, after Confucius's success at the Jiagu
Conference.

CHAPTER 4

1. Legge, *Confucius*, p.71n, notes that Zhong-du (Chung-
tû) later fell into the hands of Qi, implying that it must
have been close to the border. He disregards other
sources which claim a more central location for
Zhong-du.

2. *Liji* VII, i, 8. Müller/Legge, *Sacred Books of China*, vol.
III, p.369.

3. *Liji* VII, i, 8. Müller/Legge, *Sacred Books of China*, vol.
III, p.369.

4. *Liji* I, i, 2. Müller/Legge, *Sacred Books of China*, vol.
III, p.71. Table staff in modern times will be pleased to
know that a Confucian gentleman will never treat them
with discourtesy.

5. *Liji* I, i, 5. Müller/Legge, *Sacred Books of China*, vol.
III, p.92. This phrase is often misattributed to
Confucius himself, but he was merely quoting an older
authority.

6. *Liji* I, i, 4. Müller/Legge, *Sacred Books of China*, vol.
III, p.82.

7. Legge, *Confucius*, p.73, is not impressed, calling such
tales 'indiscriminating eulogies'. Nevertheless,
Confucius fast-tracked from the borderlands to a

government post in only a couple of years, so he must have got something right.

8. *ANA* XIII, 15.
9. Yan Hui (Yen Hûi) was also known by the scholarly name Ziyuan (Tsze-yüan). See Legge, *Confucius*, p.112.
10. *ANA* XI, 3.
11. *ANA* II, 9.
12. *ANA* VII, 10.
13. Legge, *Confucius*, p.73.
14. Legge, *Confucius*, p.73. I have altered his nineteenth-century translation slightly in the interests of clarity.
15. Legge, *Confucius*, p.74. Once again, I have amended Legge's text slightly.
16. GL, 9, i.
17. *ANA* XIII, 10. The Analects places this speech in a chapter where Confucius is journeying to Wei, implying that his 'three years' is not an objective estimate, but a lament for what he might have achieved if he had been in office for twelve more months in Lu.
18. *ANA* XIII, 11–12.
19. Yang and Yang (eds), *Records of the Historian*, p.8.
20. Two-and-a-half millennia after Confucius, Mao Zedong would famously agree: 'Political power grows out of the barrel of a gun.'
21. Chang, *Life of Confucius*, p.31, makes the logical assumption that it is the ultimate failure of this demilitarisation plan that forced Confucius to resign and leave the country, rather than the nebulous dancing-girl problem offered in most authorities. He offers no historical proof, but since almost every other story of Confucius's life is historical conjecture, I see no harm in repeating his idea here.
22. Legge, *Confucius*, p.65.

NOTES

23. Yang and Yang (eds), *Records of the Historian*, p.9. Presumably such areas were south of the Qi wall, and hence obviously on territory that was rightfully Lu's.
24. Ibid.
25. *ANA* XVIII, 6.
26. Yang and Yang (eds), *Records of the Historian*, p.9.
27. Ibid. For dates to match across different sources, it would appear that it may have taken months for the rot to set in. Brooks and Brooks (eds), *Original Analects*, however, assert that his removal from Lu was simply part of a diplomatic mission to another country, and that he never actually 'resigned'.

CHAPTER 5

1. Legge, *Mencius*, p.365, though the editor thinks this assumption is 'probably incorrect'.
2. *ANA* XIII, 9.
3. *ANA* XIV, 20. Ling, the 'Spirit Duke' was the posthumous title conferred upon Yuan, Duke of Wei, (r. 533–492 bc). See Legge, *Confucius*, p.283n.
4. *ANA* III, 24.
5. Yang and Yang (eds), *Records of the Historian*, p.10.
6. Ibid. The conspiracy theorist in me cannot resist pointing out that Confucius was 'mistaken' for Yang Hu, an officer who enjoyed a meteoric rise during a period in which Confucius was supposedly in seclusion. Could it be that the story of Yang Hu was a later concoction designed to whitewash a period in which Confucius served in office but failed?
7. Ibid.
8. van Gulik, *Sexual Life in Ancient China*, p.31.

If Confucius truly were the author of the *Spring and Autumn Annals*, he took great care to note several cases of sexual scandal, and the untimely ends that came to ministers who tried to protest; see also pp.30–2.

9. *ANA* VI, 26.
10. *ANA* XVII, 7. The warlord was Bixi (Pi Xi), who had seized control of the town of Zhong-mao (Chung-mau).
11. *ANA* XI, 25. It is a rare moment in the *Analects*, when the Master suddenly starts to sound less like a Confucian and more like a Daoist.
12. Named Jiang, ruler of Lu (r. 494–468 BC), referred to throughout this book by a translation of his posthumous title Ai, or 'Sorrowful'. In the *Liji*, Book XXIV (p.261n), Legge calls him 'the Courteous, Benevolent and Short-Lived'. The unlucky ruler was predeceased by one of his sons and his favourite wife, according to *Liji*, Book II (pp.188–9).
13. Yang and Yang (eds), *Records of the Historian*, p.15.
14. Ibid.
15. Ibid., p.16.
16. *ANA* VII, 18.
17. Yang and Yang (eds), *Records of the Historian*, p.11.
18. Ibid., p.12.
19. *ANA* V, 25.
20. *ANA* XV, 1.
21. Yang and Yang (eds), *Records of the Historian*, p.15. After this discussion, Confucius reportedly went to Chen again, but he was back by the summer.
22. Here named by his posthumous title, Chu.
23. *ANA* IX, 12. The repetition is thus in the original classical Chinese, denoting a moment of high emotion.
24. *ANA* IX, 13.

25. *ANA* XIII, 24.
26. Yang and Yang (eds), *Records of the Historian*, p.21.
27. Ibid.

CHAPTER 6

1. *ANA* IX, 2. The *Analects* does not specify a time at which this humorous exchange took place, although Yang and Yang (eds), *Records of the Historian*, p.24, place it in his twilight years.
2. *ANA* XI, 18. The strange comment is a reference to the custom of sounding a drum in order to call passers-by to listen to a recitation of a criminal's misdeeds.
3. *ANA* XI, 23.
4. *ANA* XI, 24.
5. Legge, *Confucius*, p.84.
6. Shaughnessy, *I Ching*, p.238. Confucius is also said to have been the author of a commentary on the *Yijing*, but there is no proof of this.
7. *ANA* XIV, 46.
8. Legge, *Confucius*, p.85; Yang and Yang (eds), *Records of the Historian*, p.24; Chen and Hu, *Zuo's Commentary*, p.1, 543.
9. *ANA* X, 13.
10. *Liji* II.i.3, xxi, pp.196–7.
11. A pupil of Zisi's school would become known to posterity as the philosopher Mencius.
12. Chen and Hu (eds), *Zuo's Commentary*, pp.1, 557–61, order events slightly differently.
13. Ibid., p.1, 558.
14. *ANA* XI, 8–10.
15. *ANA* VI, 9.

16. Yang and Yang (eds), *Records of the Historian*, p.25;
    Legge, *Confucius*, p.87.
17. Legge, *Confucius*, p.87.
18. Chen and Hu (eds), *Zuo's Commentary*, p.1, 560.
19. Cotterell, *The First Emperor of China*, pp.163–4.
    Although the Qin emperor infamously ordered the
    Burning of the Books, he also decreed that a single
    copy of every manuscript would be allowed to survive
    in the imperial library, for reference purposes.
    However, when the library was itself burned down in a
    later incident, the destruction of much of the
    intellectual wealth of ancient China was complete.

Further Reading

Ariel, Y., *K'ung-ts'ung-tzu – The K'ung Family Masters'
Anthology*, Princeton, Princeton University Press, 1989
Barnes, G., *The Rise of Civilization in East Asia: The
Archaeology of China, Korea and Japan*, London, Thames
& Hudson, 1999
Brooks, E. and Taeko Brooks (eds), *The Original Analects:
Sayings of Confucius and His Successors*, New York,
Columbia University Press, 1997
Chang, C., *A Life of Confucius*, Taipei, Hwakang Press, 1971
Chen, K. and Hu Zhihui (eds), *Zuo's Commentary*,
Changsha, Hunan People's Press, 1997
Cleary, T., *The Essential Confucius*, New York, Castle Books,
1992
Clements, J., *The Little Book of Chinese Proverbs*, Bath,
Siena, 1999
Cotterell, A., *The First Emperor of China*, London,
Macmillan, 1981
Dawson, R., *Confucius,* Oxford, Oxford University Press, 1981
Fu, J. and Chen Songchang, *Mawangdui Han mu wenwu:
Cultural Relics Unearthed from the Han Tombs at
Mawangdui*, Changsha, Hunan Press, 1992

Ikeda, T., '*Maötei Kan bo hakusho Shüeki Yö hen no Kenkyü* [Researches into the Scroll *Essentials of the Yijing* from the Han Dynasty Tomb at Mawangdui]', *Töyö Bunka*, 123 (1994), pp.111–207

Knoblock, J. and Jeffrey Riegel (eds), *The Annals of Lü Buwei: A Complete Translation and Study*, Stanford, Stanford University Press, 2000

Kramers, R., *K'ung Tzu Chia Yü: The School Sayings of Confucius* [*Kongzi Jiayu a.k.a Narratives of the School*], Leiden, E.J. Brill, 1950

Legge, J. (ed.) (1893), *Confucius: Confucian Analects, The Great Learning and the Doctrine of the Mean, Translated with Critical and Exegetical Notes, Prolegomena, Copious Indexes and Dictionary of All Characters*, New York, Dover (1971 reprint)

——, *The Works of Mencius*, Oxford, Clarendon Press, 1895

Luo, C. et al., *Kongzi Mingyan: A Collection of Confucius' Sayings*, Jinan, Qi Lu Press, 1988

Müller, M. (ed.) (1885), *Sacred Books of China, Vol. III and IV – The Li Ki* (*Liji – Book of Rites*), trans. James Legge, Delhi, Motilal Banarsidass (1966 reprint)

Sertori, J., *The Little Book of Feng Shui*, Bath, Siena, 1998

Shaughnessy, E., *I Ching: The Classic of Changes*, New York, Ballantine, 1996

Sims, B., *Confucius*, London, Franklin Watts, 1968

van Gulik, R., *Sexual Life in Ancient China*, Leiden, E.J. Brill, 1974

Xin, G., *Lunyu: Analects of Confucius*, Beijing, Sinolingua, 1994

Yang, H. and Gladys Yang (eds), *Records of the Historian, Written by Szuma Chien*, Beijing, Commercial Press, 1974

Yao, X., *An Introduction to Confucianism*, Cambridge, Cambridge University Press, 2000

Index

135

BY THE SAME AUTHOR

**Pirate King: Coxinga and the Fall of the
Ming Dynasty**

Coxinga, son of a samurai mother and China's richest
smuggler, became one of the last warriors loyal to the
doomed Ming emperor, commanding a fleet of 3,000
ships and over 250,000 soldiers. When the Ming dynasty
fell to the Manchus in 1644, Coxinga turned to piracy,
ousting the Dutch from Taiwan to become ruler of the
island. He was later made a god – twice. This riveting
book tells the incredible story of this infamous pirate king
in full for the first time.

ISBN 0-7509-3269-4
Hardback
288pp